T0194663

An Analysis of

W. Chan Kim and Renée Mauborgne's

Blue Ocean Strategy

Andreas Mebert
with
Stephanie Lowe

Published by Macat International Ltd
24:13 Coda Centre, 189 Munster Road, London SW6 6AW.

Distributed exclusively by Routledge
2 Park Square, Milton Park, Abingdon, Oxon OX14 4RN
711 Third Avenue, New York, NY 10017, USA

Routledge is an imprint of the Taylor & Francis Group, an informa business

www.macat.com
info@macat.com

Cataloguing in Publication Data
A catalogue record for this book is available from the British Library.
Library of Congress Cataloguing-in-Publication Data is available upon request.
Cover illustration: Etienne Gilfillan

ISBN 978-1-912302-13-0 (hardback)
ISBN 978-1-912128-42-6 (paperback)
ISBN 978-1-912281-01-5 (e-book)

Notice
The information in this book is designed to orientate readers of the work under analysis,
to elucidate and contextualise its key ideas and themes, and to aid in the development
of critical thinking skills. It is not meant to be used, nor should it be used, as a
substitute for original thinking or in place of original writing or research. References and
notes are provided for informational purposes and their presence does not constitute
endorsement of the information or opinions therein. This book is presented solely for
educational purposes. It is sold on the understanding that the publisher is not engaged
to provide any scholarly advice. The publisher has made every effort to ensure that
this book is accurate and up-to-date, but makes no warranties or representations with
regard to the completeness or reliability of the information it contains. The information
and the opinions provided herein are not guaranteed or warranted to produce particular
results and may not be suitable for students of every ability. The publisher shall not be
liable for any loss, damage or disruption arising from any errors or omissions, or from
the use of this book, including, but not limited to, special, incidental, consequential or
other damages caused, or alleged to have been caused, directly or indirectly, by the
information contained within.

CONTENTS

THE MACAT LIBRARY

The Macat Library is a series of unique academic explorations of seminal works in the humanities and social sciences – books and papers that have had a significant and widely recognised impact on their disciplines. It has been created to serve as much more than just a summary of what lies between the covers of a great book. It illuminates and explores the influences on, ideas of, and impact of that book. Our goal is to offer a learning resource that encourages critical thinking and fosters a better, deeper understanding of important ideas.

Each publication is divided into three Sections: Influences, Ideas, and Impact. Each Section has four Modules. These explore every important facet of the work, and the responses to it.

This Section-Module structure makes a Macat Library book easy to use, but it has another important feature. Because each Macat book is written to the same format, it is possible (and encouraged!) to cross-reference multiple Macat books along the same lines of inquiry or research. This allows the reader to open up interesting interdisciplinary pathways.

To further aid your reading, lists of glossary terms and people mentioned are included at the end of this book (these are indicated by an asterisk [*] throughout) – as well as a list of works cited.

Macat has worked with the University of Cambridge to identify the elements of critical thinking and understand the ways in which six different skills combine to enable effective thinking.
Three allow us to fully understand a problem; three more give us the tools to solve it. Together, these six skills make up the **PACIER** model of critical thinking. They are:

ANALYSIS – understanding how an argument is built
EVALUATION – exploring the strengths and weaknesses of an argument
INTERPRETATION – understanding issues of meaning

CREATIVE THINKING – coming up with new ideas and fresh connections
PROBLEM-SOLVING – producing strong solutions
REASONING – creating strong arguments

To find out more, visit **WWW.MACAT.COM.**

CRITICAL THINKING AND *BLUE OCEAN STRATEGY*

Primary critical thinking skill: CREATIVE THINKING
Secondary critical thinking skill: ANALYSIS

In *Blue Ocean Strategy,* W. Chan Kim and Renée Mauborgne tackle the central problem facing all businesses: how to perform better than your competitors? Their solution involves taking a creative approach to the normal view of competition.

In the normal framework, competition is a zero-sum game: if there are two companies competing for the same market, as one does better, the other has to do worse. The authors' creative leap is to suggest one can beat the competition by not competing. Companies should avoid confronting competitors in crowded marketplaces, what they call 'red oceans,' and instead seek out new markets, or 'blue oceans.' Once the blue oceans have been identified, companies can get down to the task of creating unique products which exploit that market.

Chan and Mauborgne argue, for example, that a wine company might decide to start appealing to a group previously uninterested in wine. This would be a 'blue ocean' market, giving the winemaker a huge advantage, which they could exploit by creating a wine that appealed to the tastes of a beer-drinking demographic. A classic of business writing, *Blue Ocean Strategy* is creative thinking and problem solving at its best.

ABOUT THE AUTHORS OF THE ORIGINAL WORK

W. Chan Kim was born in South Korea in 1952. He was educated in the United States at the University of Michigan's Ross School of Business, where he completed his studies and began his academic career.

Renée Mauborgne was born in the United States in 1963 and completed studies at Harvard University followed by the University of Michigan's Ross School of Business, where she first met Kim. Mauborgne is a distinguished fellow and professor of strategy at INSEAD business school in Fontainebleau, France. Kim also teaches at INSEAD, and currently serves as a fellow at the World Economic Forum. Together, they are co-directors of the INSEAD Blue Ocean Strategy Institute.

ABOUT THE AUTHORS OF THE ANALYSIS

Dr Andreas Mebert holds a PhD in business administration from the University of Manchester.

Stephanie Lowe holds an MSc in global media and journalism from the London School of Economics.

ABOUT MACAT

GREAT WORKS FOR CRITICAL THINKING

Macat is focused on making the ideas of the world's great thinkers accessible and comprehensible to everybody, everywhere, in ways that promote the development of enhanced critical thinking skills.

It works with leading academics from the world's top universities to produce new analyses that focus on the ideas and the impact of the most influential works ever written across a wide variety of academic disciplines. Each of the works that sit at the heart of its growing library is an enduring example of great thinking. But by setting them in context – and looking at the influences that shaped their authors, as well as the responses they provoked – Macat encourages readers to look at these classics and game-changers with fresh eyes. Readers learn to think, engage and challenge their ideas, rather than simply accepting them.

'Macat offers an amazing first-of-its-kind tool for interdisciplinary learning and research. Its focus on works that transformed their disciplines and its rigorous approach, drawing on the world's leading experts and educational institutions, opens up a world-class education to anyone.'

Andreas Schleicher
Director for Education and Skills, Organisation for Economic
Co-operation and Development

'Macat is taking on some of the major challenges in university education ... They have drawn together a strong team of active academics who are producing teaching materials that are novel in the breadth of their approach.'

Prof Lord Broers,
former Vice-Chancellor of the University of Cambridge

'The Macat vision is exceptionally exciting. It focuses upon new modes of learning which analyse and explain seminal texts which have profoundly influenced world thinking and so social and economic development. It promotes the kind of critical thinking which is essential for any society and economy.
This is the learning of the future.'

Rt Hon Charles Clarke, former UK Secretary of State for Education

'The Macat analyses provide immediate access to the critical conversation surrounding the books that have shaped their respective discipline, which will make them an invaluable resource to all of those, students and teachers, working in the field.'

Professor William Tronzo, University of California at San Diego

WAYS IN TO THE TEXT

KEY POINTS

- W. Chan Kim is a Korean-born business scholar who currently teaches at the business school INSEAD* in France. His co-author, Renée Mauborgne, is an American business scholar and a professor of strategy at INSEAD who has collaborated with Kim on several projects.

- *Blue Ocean Strategy* argues that in very competitive environments, companies should seek out "blue oceans"*— uncontested market space—in order to grow.

- *Blue Ocean Strategy* is presented as a practical guide for managers and students; it includes numerous examples and learning frameworks.

Who Are W. Chan Kim and Renée Mauborgne?

W. Chan Kim and Renée Mauborgne coauthored the book *Blue Ocean Strategy: How to Create Uncontested Market Space and Make the Competition Irrelevant* (2005). Kim, a native of South Korea, immigrated to the United States in the 1970s and attended the University of Michigan's Ross School of Business,* where he would later teach. There he met Mauborgne, a student at the school and graduate of Harvard University; this led to a lasting collaboration. *Blue Ocean Strategy* was a product of their shared research while at the business school INSEAD, where Kim and Mauborgne still teach.

Kim and Mauborgne's institutional affiliation helped shape the ideas introduced in *Blue Ocean Strategy*. Located in Fontainebleau, France, the business school INSEAD is known for educating managers of many of the world's largest corporations, a few of which also funded the authors' research for this book. This led Kim and Mauborgne to adopt the perspective that large multinational corporations, as opposed to entrepreneurs (individuals in business), can ultimately develop a useful strategy to sidestep saturated markets by developing alternatives around the needs of consumers or a target market.

In *Blue Ocean Strategy*, Kim and Mauborgne pioneer a new strategy for innovation in so-called "red-ocean"* market conditions—that is, overly saturated markets where too much competition leads to a glut of supply* and weak demand.* The authors' perspective on these markets evolved from their close relationship with the business community. *Blue Ocean Strategy* was written at a time when globalization* and technological innovation had produced highly integrated world markets, resulting in many companies facing rich competition for customers.

What Does *Blue Ocean Strategy* Say?

Blue Ocean Strategy argues that companies facing red oceans (strong competition in existing markets) should seek out blue oceans (new markets) in order to grow. Much of the book deals with how companies can identify these blue oceans to create unique products. In economics, competition* refers to the rivalry among sellers trying to increase profits,* market share, and sales volume by varying the elements of the marketing mix—in terms of price, product, distribution, and promotion.

This conclusion—that companies should seek new markets, or attempt to make competition irrelevant by sidestepping it—diverges from traditional views of market competition that exists simply in ecosystems of a zero-sum game* (that is, business environments in which one company's success is another's failure). In Kim and Mauborge's framework, however, this need not be the case. The authors call for "more entrepreneurial" managers (that is, roughly, managers who are more ambitious and imaginative in business matters) to create concrete tools or frameworks to help their teams undergo a step-by-step process that implements a blue ocean strategy in their work.

The book, much of which was originally published in a series of articles in the *Harvard Business Review*, represents the culmination of ten years of research in strategic management that centers on value innovation.*

Value innovation forms the core feature of a blue ocean strategy, and can be loosely defined as the attempt to identify and build aspects of a business that make it competitive—or transcend marketplace competition. For example, the authors give the example of the Canadian entertainment company Cirque du Soleil,* which innovated by bringing together the excitement of the circus with the intellectual gravitas of the theater. Rather than compete with other circus companies, Cirque du Soleil created its own market space. The authors argue that by pursuing such innovation, companies can avoid what they call "the value-cost trade-off"*—that is, most business executives assume that investing in a company's value increases its costs. In contrast, the authors suggest companies can pursue both value and cost-effectiveness if they operate in blue oceans rather than red oceans.

Blue Ocean Strategy also includes several frameworks for companies to help them move towards blue oceans. For example, their "Four Actions Framework" is designed to help managers identify and take actions that can help them build value and eventually spot a blue ocean. In essence, the framework consists of four questions:

- What can be eliminated from the market?
- What can be reduced?

- What must be raised?
- What must be created?[1]

By answering these questions and relating them to the company's business, managers will discover future directions that can add value. As an example, the authors discuss the Australian wine-producers Casella Wines, the producers of the Australian wine brand Yellow Tail.* With Yellow Tail, the company created a blue ocean by identifying the popular taste features and consumer preferences of non-wine drinkers, such as those who drank beer, and developed a wine range with adjusted characteristics that incorporated some of those features.

Why Does *Blue Ocean Strategy* Matter?

The ideas presented in the international best seller *Blue Ocean Strategy* can aid a broad readership in understanding and evaluating key problems around greater themes of competition and market creation. Red oceans can be thought of as crowded, bloodied waters: they represent a paradigm (a conceptual model or world view) that has dominated commerce and the marketplace for generations. Even today, many businesses and managers assume that in a space filled with similar products or services, they can gain the upper hand by battling with the competition at every turn. But in their book, Kim and Mauborgne outline an entirely different and compelling course. If managers and businesses create products unique in all the marketplace—whether by seeking out overlooked consumers (as the Yellow Tail brand did) or combining old categories in new ways (as Cirque du Soleil did)—they will own the newly created space and effectively sail on a wide-open "blue ocean."

Kim and Mauborgne emphasize that new businesses must act as risk* takers, while they also highlight the benefits of a first-mover advantage*—the competitive advantage that arises from the control of resources when one is first to the market.

The authors believe new market creation can both cure lagging profitability and create tools and frameworks where students and business practitioners can grasp key concepts around innovation and the creation of value—even as they evaluate and identify associated key problems. Mainly, the authors' concept of malleable market boundaries draws on the work of the Austrian American economist Joseph Schumpeter.*[2] According to his thesis, entrepreneurs can create market growth from within a market as opposed to outside it. Kim and Mauborgne's approach to the concept of value creation* (the primary objective of all businesses) is key in understanding how new markets (blue oceans) render saturated old markets (red oceans) irrelevant.

While some argue that the prevailing ideas presented in *Blue Ocean Strategy* are not new, the book has revitalized interest in practical tools that can be used as a step-to-step guide in generating new market ideas. The theories in *Blue Ocean Strategy* also offer students in non-business disciplines a way to broaden their skills by introducing new methodologies to their study. Kim and Mauborgne pay particular attention to the question of how to respond to overcrowding in the marketplace. The frameworks they provide result in a timeless yet practical approach that offers smart solutions to the challenges posed by future periods of low growth.

In many ways, Kim and Mauborgne help readers to better understand the world around them because they emphasize practice over theory. The book proposes that new market creation solves and even avoids the problem of hotly contested market spaces. While monopolies in newly created markets can only ever be temporary—the smartphone arena comes to mind—Kim and Mauborgne view their own reconstructionist* approach, according to which a market can be reconstructed by entrepreneurs from within their position of advantage, as a continuation in strategy. The authors argue that competition will eventually make way for new ventures in newly created markets.

This sort of mindset is especially appropriate if a market is to be expanded in a new way through the actions of a visionary company.

NOTES

1   W. Chan Kim and Renée Mauborgne, *Blue Ocean Strategy: How to Create Uncontested Market Space and Make the Competition Irrelevant* (Boston: Harvard Business Press, 2005), 29.

2   Joseph A. Schumpeter, *Capitalism, Socialism and Democracy* (London: Taylor and Francis, 1942).

SECTION 1
INFLUENCES

MODULE 1
THE AUTHOR AND THE HISTORICAL CONTEXT

KEY POINTS

- *Blue Ocean Strategy* is a guidebook for creating value in new business environments, which remains important in today's rapidly changing commercial climate.

- Kim and Mauborgne met when Mauborgne was his student, and their work together has been deeply influenced by the practical problem- solving approach taught at the University of Michigan's Ross School of Business.*

- The book was shaped, most importantly, by the authors' analysis of markets defined by an over-abundance of competition* (market saturation),* a state that made it difficult for businesses to compete in traditional ways.

Why Read This Text?

In *Blue Ocean Strategy: How to Create Uncontested Market Space and Make the Competition Irrelevant* (2005), W. Chan Kim and Renée Mauborgne outline a strategy intended to help managers escape low-growth markets where companies conduct competitive battles over market share with their business rivals in a zero-sum game* (a situation where one company's success means another company's loss).

The authors suggest that instead of competing in such markets, companies should provide innovative value to new groups of consumers in new markets where competition is irrelevant. In their analysis of 150 strategic moves, Kim and Mauborgne discovered a pattern among companies that managed to avoid traditional competition. *Blue Ocean Strategy* discusses their insights from this

> 66 This is a book about friendship, about loyalty, about believing in one another. It was because of that friendship, and that belief, that we set out on the journey to explore the ideas in the book and eventually came to write it. 99
>
> W. Chan Kim and Renée Mauborgne, *Blue Ocean Strategy: How to Create Uncontested Market Space and Make the Competition Irrelevant*

research, showing how any company can implement a strategy that bypasses competition and increases profits.* In so doing, *Blue Ocean Strategy* provides valuable advice and guidance for managers and students of business strategy.* Three and a half million copies of the book have been sold, and it is listed among the world's most popular business books. The approach discussed in the book revolves around a key component of value innovation*—an important aspect of today's business environment.

The title *Blue Ocean Strategy* comes from the metaphor of a blue ocean* that appears throughout the book. Markets in which companies compete with one another are called red oceans,*[1] where the color red refers to the metaphorical "blood" that companies draw from one another as they struggle for market share. By contrast, a blue ocean is a market that no competitors have yet entered and is therefore free from the "blood" of competition.

Authors' Lives

W. Chan Kim was born in South Korea in 1952. He was educated at the University of Michigan's Ross School of Business, where he finished his studies in the late 1970s and began his academic career. He is currently a fellow of the World Economic Forum* and co-director of the INSEAD Blue Ocean Strategy Institute.* Renée Mauborgne was born in the United States and educated at Harvard University and later the University of Michigan, where she eventually met her professor—and co-author—W. Chan Kim.[2] As they write in the book: "We met twenty years ago in a classroom—one the professor, the other the student. And we have worked together ever since, often seeing ourselves along the journey as two wet rats in a drain."[3]

The Ross School of Business is famous for its Multidisciplinary Action Projects approach (MAP),* which encourages students to take practical paths to solving actual business problems.[4] Even though this approach was officially adopted in 1990, just two years before Kim and Mauborgne left to accept their current positions at the INSEAD business school* in France, their research seemed influenced by the MAP's emphasis on practically applicable business theory. Indeed, Kim and Mauborgne acknowledge that they specifically developed and tested the managerial tools in *Blue Ocean Strategy* with practical problem-solving in mind.

Authors' Background

When *Blue Ocean Strategy* was written, companies faced saturated markets, meaning the majority of companies produced a supply* of goods and services that surpassed demand.* This change was due to an increase in industrial productivity and spurred by globalization,* the process by which markets are opened up to new technologies and competition across international borders. As the authors write: "Accelerated technological advances have substantially improved industrial productivity and have allowed suppliers to produce an unprecedented array of products and services."[5] This resulted in a lack of differentiation* between products (that is, a marketplace defined by overly similar products) within single industries, along with price wars* between competitors and shrinking profit margins (total revenue when the various costs of business have been deducted). The authors felt a need to address these so-called red ocean market conditions in their work.

The authors' institutional affiliation also helped to shape the ideas put forth in *Blue Ocean Strategy*. As mentioned, Kim and Mauborgne wrote their text at the business school INSEAD, which is famous for educating managers in many of the world's largest corporations. Some of these corporations, including the Boston Consulting Group,* funded the authors' research,[6] which may have led Kim and Mauborgne to adopt the perspective of large multinational corporations—rather than, for example, entrepreneurs. And though entrepreneurs could arguably learn much from *Blue Ocean Strategy*, it serves mainly as a guide for large companies seeking to overcome the boundaries of saturated markets.

NOTES

1   Kim W. Chan and Renée Mauborgne, *Blue Ocean Strategy: How to Create Uncontested Market Space and Make the Competition Irrelevant* (Boston: Harvard Business Press, 2005), 4.

2   Stuart Crainer, "W. Chan Kim and Renée Mauborgne: The Thought Leader Interview," accessed October 8, 2013, http://www.strategy-business.com/article/11695?gko=d33f3.

3   Kim and Mauborgne, *Blue Ocean Strategy*, ix.

4   University of Michigan's Ross School of Business, "Multidisciplinary Action Projects (MAP)," accessed October 22, 2013, http://michiganross.umich.edu/programs/map.

5   Kim and Mauborgne, *Blue Ocean Strategy*, 8.

6   Kim and Mauborgne, *Blue Ocean Strategy*, xiv.

MODULE 2
ACADEMIC CONTEXT

KEY POINTS

- Business strategy* as a field is concerned with how to make smart decisions in various business situations, particularly in the face of uncertainty and competitive threats.

- Strategic thinking traces back to the writing of the Chinese general Sun Tzu,* author of the classic military treatise *The Art of War*, and has more recently evolved to encompass many aspects of the business process.

- Kim and Mauborgne situate themselves in a somewhat artificial dichotomy (that is, contrasting possibilities defined by opposition) between what they call the "reconstructionist"* view of strategy, according to which a market can be internally reconstructed through entrepreneurship to the benefit of that entrepreneur, and the structuralist* perspective, according to which only external forces can change a market.

The Work in its Context

W. Chan Kim and Renée Mauborgne's *Blue Ocean Strategy: How to Create Uncontested Market Space and Make the Competition Irrelevant* is part of a larger literature on business strategy. At the most general level, business strategy concerns itself with building theories and models that enable businesses and other strategic entities (such as militaries and politicians) to make better decisions. Strategy consists of a plan to achieve a specific goal; by analyzing various planning techniques for effectiveness, insights emerge that help to form practical strategic frameworks. Today, most work on strategy is dedicated to business

> **❝ Ponder and deliberate before you make a move. ❞**
> Sun Tzu, *The Art of War*

situations—but historically, strategic thinking formed the backbone of military planning and combat.

In 1962, the Harvard professor Alfred Chandler* defined the field of business strategy as follows: "Strategy is the determination of the basic long-term goals of an enterprise, and the adoption of courses of action and the allocation of resources necessary for carrying out these goals."[1]

Notice how this definition zeroes in on the creation of practical guides to implement strategies—and not merely the study of past behavior. A later definition comes from the Harvard business professor Michael Porter,* who called strategy the "broad formula for how a business is going to compete, what its goals should be, and what policies will be needed to carry out those goals."[2] Porter emphasizes the use of strategy within a business, and this serves as perhaps the one key concept that informs *Blue Ocean Strategy*: a book explicitly concerned with strategies related to competition.*

Overview of the Field

Perhaps the earliest work dedicated to strategy is *The Art of War*, written by the Chinese general Sun Tzu in the sixth century B.C.E. Specifically written with military interactions in mind, this ancient book describes how armies should manage their troops and engage their opponents. Crucially, *The Art of War* emphasizes the importance of responding to changing circumstances and uncertainty. For example, Sun Tzu writes in the section on "Maneuvering": "The difficulty of tactical maneuvering consists in turning the devious into the direct, and misfortune into gain."[3]

In the early 1900s, as the global economy became more industrial and technological, strategy literature became concerned with "pushing the boundaries of industrialization and operations."[4] One of the important books at this time was the pioneering management consultant Frederick Winslow Taylor's* *The Principles of Scientific Management*, which advanced the idea that workers should be as efficient as possible to increase productivity. As Taylor writes: "In the case of a more complicated manufacturing establishment, it should … be perfectly clear that the greatest permanent prosperity for the workman, coupled with the greatest prosperity for the employer, can be brought about only when the work of the establishment is done with the smallest combined expenditure of human effort, plus nature's cost, plus the cost for the use of capital in the shape of machines, buildings, etc."[5]

Beginning in the 1970s and through the 1990s, a more holistic approach to strategy (that is, an approach that considered the ways in which the context and constituent parts of a business's strategy functioned together) gradually replaced Taylor's focus on efficiency. In 1985, Michael Porter developed the idea of using strategy to create product differentiation* (developing a product that can be marketed as being unlike other products) and value at different stages of production.[6] Many works followed Porter's lead, including a *Harvard Business Review* article by the corporate strategists C. K. Prahalad* and Gary Hamel* that highlighted the importance of looking for competitive advantages—not only in the business environment at large but within an organization as well.[7] And another important work, the influential business consultant John Kotter's* *Leading Change*, discussed techniques for implementing change efforts within large organizations.[8] According to the consulting firm A. T. Kearney,* "During this period, strategy became a proper discipline: more stand-alone, more analytical, and more cerebral."[9]

Academic Influences

Kim and Mauborgne make little mention of the general strategy debates listed above, but rather place their analysis in a hypothetical dispute between what they call the reconstructionist view and structuralism.* Specifically, they characterize reconstructionism as a response to—and a rejection of—structuralist thought, according to which, Kim and Mauborgne argue, a market's structure is unchangeable.

Importantly, these schools of thought did not exist in business scholarship, but, rather, appear to be concepts the authors redefined and adopted for this book. For Kim and Mauborgne, structuralism's roots lie in industrial organization economics, which sees market forces (that is, the supply* of goods and services and the consumer's demand* for these goods and services) as ultimately determining the conduct of buyers and sellers. According to the authors, structuralists believe that only forces external to the market such as changes in government regulation or cultural movements can alter a market's structure or boundaries. Reconstructionists, by contrast, reject this view—and Kim and Mauborgne position themselves in the latter camp.

The authors trace the origins of reconstructionism to the influential economist Joseph Schumpeter's* theory of entrepreneurial innovation. Schumpeter views entrepreneurs as possessing the power to change and grow markets from within. Kim and Mauborgne argue that the "new growth theory"* developed by the economist and entrepreneur Paul Romer* took Schumpeter's argument of innovation by a lone entrepreneur to a system-wide level. Romer places growth in the context of other human needs and contends that innovation inside a market can be replicated by the entire market once its patterns are understood.[10]

Kim and Mauborgne assert that any organization in any market can carry out the innovation process simply by restructuring the market data and elements in a fundamentally new way.[11] Hence, the authors position themselves as part of a counter-movement within the field of strategy—a stance that in and of itself has compelling strategic implications.

NOTES

1   Alfred Chandler, *Strategy and Structure: Chapters in the History of the American Industrial Enterprise* (Washington, DC: Beard Books, 2003), 13.

2   Michael E. Porter, *Competitive Strategy: Techniques for Analyzing Industries and Competitors* (New York: Free Press, 1980), preface.

3   Sun Tzu, "The Art of War," Project Gutenberg, 1994: chapter 7, Sun-Tzu Reference Archive (2000), www.marxists.org/reference/archive/sun-tzu/works/art-of-war/ch07.htm.

4   Johan Aurik et al., "The History of Strategy and its Future Prospects," *A.T. Kearney*, accessed June 15, 2015, https://www.atkearney.com/documents/10192/4260571/History+of+Strategy+and+Its+Future+Prospects.pdf/ 29f8c6e8-7cdb-4a25-8acc-b0c39e4439e1.

5   Frederick Winslow Taylor, *The Principles of Scientific Management* (Mineola, New York: Dover Publications, 1997), 2.

6   Michael E. Porter, *Competitive Advantage: Creating and Sustaining Superior Performance* (New York: Free Press, 1985).

7   C. K. Prahalad and Gary Hamel, "The Core Competence of the Corporation," *Harvard Business Review* (May-June 1990).

8   John P. Kotter, *Leading Change* (Harvard Business Review Press, 1996).

9   Aurik et al., "The History of Strategy and its Future Prospects."

10 Paul Romer, "The Origins of Endogenous Growth," *The Journal of Economic Perspectives* 8 (1994): 3–22.

11 Kim W. Chan and Renée Mauborgne, *Blue Ocean Strategy: How to Create Uncontested Market Space and Make the Competition Irrelevant* (Boston: Harvard Business Press, 2005), 209–10.

MODULE 3
THE PROBLEM

KEY POINTS

- Kim and Mauborgne wrote *Blue Ocean Strategy* at a time when strategy scholars were considering how to grow businesses in a saturated environment.

- The authors of *Blue Ocean Strategy* were inspired to write the book by the limitations they observed in previous books that described how companies can grow.

- Kim and Mauborgne developed their ideas largely outside of contemporary debate and focused primarily on reaching a business audience.

Core Question

W. Chan Kim and Renée Mauborgne wrote *Blue Ocean Strategy* in the context of rapidly changing business conditions due to globalization,* the process by which markets are opened across international borders, which led to the saturation* of markets (that is, markets defined by a surplus of competition)* and the spread of business services worldwide. Accordingly, the key questions that Kim and Mauborgne try to answer in the book are:

- How can a company break out of the red ocean* of bloody competition?
- How can it create a blue ocean*?
- Is there a systematic approach to achieving and thereby sustaining high performance?[1]

These questions become particularly relevant when one considers the nature and tone of the contemporary business environment.

> ❝ As red oceans become increasingly bloody, management will need to be more concerned with blue oceans than the current cohort of managers is accustomed to. ❞
>
> W. Chan Kim and Renée Mauborgne, *Blue Ocean Strategy: How to Create Uncontested Market Space and Make the Competition Irrelevant*

Beyond vague calls for managers to be more entrepreneurial, few if any tools or frameworks existed to help managers develop and implement a blue ocean strategy, step by step. This contrasts sharply with the multitude of competitive and for-profit* frameworks that academic business literature has developed for companies to succeed in so-called red oceans; examples are the influential Five Forces* and Generic Strategies* approaches proposed by the Harvard business professor Michael Porter,* both of which offer tools useful to approaching the problem of competition within one's customary market. One popular business book of 2005 was practically a red ocean manifesto: Harvey Mackay's *Swim With the Sharks Without Being Eaten Alive.*[2]

Rejecting popular opinion, *Blue Ocean Strategy*—also published in 2005—took an opposing point of view and addressed a wide knowledge gap in the process.

Kim and Mauborgne explain the concept of the blue ocean strategy, and what it can accomplish, by using examples from their research. They then tackle the question of how to create a blue ocean by providing a number of frameworks that form a practical instruction manual for managers to formulate and execute a blue ocean strategy.

The Participants

Kim and Mauborgne mention two sources of inspiration for the research that underlies *Blue Ocean Strategy*: The American business writers Tom Peters* and Robert H. Waterman Jr.'s* *In Search of Excellence*,[3] and the business analysts James C. Collins* and Jerry I. Porras's* *Built to Last*.[4] Both books (published in 1982 and 1994, respectively) attempted to show how companies attain strong, profitable growth. Kim and Mauborgne, however, felt these works failed to provide satisfactory answers, as most of the companies those authors mentioned did not remain financially successful. As Kim and Mauborgne say: "For those sample companies in the book *Built to Last* … it was later found that if industry performance was removed from the equation, many of the companies in *Built to Last* were no longer exceptionally excellent."[5]

The authors concluded that focusing on a company as the unit of analysis was an incorrect way to investigate growth strategy—after all, some companies may succeed for a period due to unobserved factors. Rather, they decided that the "strategic move" is the proper "unit of analysis for explaining the creation of blue oceans and the root of profitable growth."[6] This shift in perspective led the authors towards the framework and substance of *Blue Ocean Strategy*.

The Contemporary Debate

Kim and Mauborgne have had relatively little interaction with mainstream academic debate and very rarely mention other academic works in their book, mostly relying on their own examples and research. As both authors are prominent business scholars, they likely knew of other writings on innovation in new markets, both inside and outside academia, but their book does not make this association clear.

In the non-academic business community, however, *Blue Ocean Strategy* has enjoyed tremendous success. It has topped bestseller lists, won numerous awards, and been translated into 43 languages—many observers consider it one of the most successful business books of all time.[7] Some scholarly studies that explored the validity of the book's claims have concluded that indeed, they can be successfully implemented.[8] Nevertheless, their broad validity has yet to be confirmed, and even Kim and Mauborgne have implied that the new, uncontested markets they urge managers to create will likely turn crowded and hotly contested after a certain amount of time.[9]

The best way to view the contemporary debate surrounding *Blue Ocean Strategy* is perhaps not through the lens of academia but from the perspective of the business community at large—and specifically, how large companies use and influence it.

NOTES

1   Kim W. Chan and Renée Mauborgne, *Blue Ocean Strategy: How to Create Uncontested Market Space and Make the Competition Irrelevant* (Boston: Harvard Business Press, 2005), 9.

2   Harvey Mackay, *Swim With the Sharks Without Being Eaten Alive* (New York: HarperBusiness Essentials, 2005).

3   Thomas J. Peters and Robert H. Waterman Jr., *In Search of Excellence: Lessons from America's Best-Run Companies* (New York: Harper & Row, 1982).

4   James C. Collins and Jerry I. Porras, *Built to Last: Successful Habits of Visionary Companies* (New York: Harper Business, 1994).

5   *Blue Ocean Strategy*, "A Conversation with W. Chan Kim and Renée Mauborgne," accessed June 20, 2015, http://www.blueoceanstrategy.com/wp-content/uploads/2013/06/AuthorsQandA.pdf.

6   *Blue Ocean Strategy*, "A Conversation with W. Chan Kim and Renée Mauborgne."

7   *Blue Ocean Strategy*, "Awards," accessed October 8, 2013, http://www.blueoceanstrategy.com/awards/.

8   Emiel F. M. Wubben et al., "Finding Uncontested Markets for European Fruit and Vegetables Through Applying the Blue Ocean Strategy," *British Food Journal* 114 (2012): 248–71; Dennis Pitta, "Issues in a Down Economy: Blue Oceans and New Product Development," *Journal of Product and Brand Management* 18 (2009): 292–6.

9   Kim and Mauborgne, *Blue Ocean Strategy*, 5.

MODULE 4
THE AUTHOR'S CONTRIBUTION

KEY POINTS

- The authors of *Blue Ocean Strategy* set out to change the way business leaders think about competition.*

- Kim and Mauborgne attempted to carry out this goal by analyzing a sample of several companies and their leadership strategies.

- Kim and Mauborgne built on their own work in three papers that preceded the publication of *Blue Ocean Strategy*.

Author's Aims

In writing *Blue Ocean Strategy*, W. Chan Kim and Renée Mauborgne set out to meet three objectives:

- to convince readers that attempting to create blue oceans* is worthwhile and desirable
- to furnish readers with the practical tools necessary to put this approach into practice
- to provide an alternative to the mainstream approach to competition that has become conventional wisdom in the field of business strategy. *

Towards these ends, the book is divided into three parts that each correspond to one of these aims.

On a fundamental level, *Blue Ocean Strategy* set out to change the way academics thought about competition. Specifically, the authors wanted to answer the following question: how can businesses succeed without competing in so-called red oceans?* In posing this question, *Blue Ocean Strategy* runs counter to the work of influential thinkers

> ❝ Our aim is to make the formulation and execution of blue ocean strategies as systematic and actionable as competing in the red waters of known market space. Only then can companies step up to the challenge of creating blue oceans in a smart and responsible way that is both opportunity maximizing and risk minimizing. ❞
>
> W. Chan Kim and Renée Mauborgne, *Blue Ocean Strategy: How to Create Uncontested Market Space and Make the Competition Irrelevant*

such as the business strategists Michael Porter* and Jorge Vasconcellos e Sá,* whose analysis focuses on how to beat the competition. Vasconcellos e Sá, for example, draws inspiration from military theories, projecting these onto business contexts to propose strategies for attacking the competition. Similarly, Michael Porter's influential "Five Forces"* and "Generic Strategies"* frameworks focus on confronting competition within one's customary market.[1] In *Blue Ocean Strategy,* Kim and Mauborgne question this incessant focus on competition as a means for achieving profit* growth, and propose a different approach.

Approach

The authors of *Blue Ocean Strategy* identify strategic behaviors (or moves) "that have delivered products and services that opened and captured new market space, with a significant leap in demand."[*2] By looking systematically at these "moves," the authors sought to "understand the pattern by which blue oceans are created and captured and high performance is achieved."[3] These strategic moves can include actions that introduce new products, marketing campaigns, and changes to the production process.

In the first phase of this research, Kim and Mauborgne examined a sample of 108 product launches. They found that while only a minority of these products were entirely innovative and cutting-edge—14 percent—these products were far more profitable than the other 86 percent, which were merely line extensions (new products introduced under existing brand names).[4] This observation prompted the authors to analyze 150 strategic moves from both successful and unsuccessful companies from various industries between 1880 and 2000. Ultimately the authors concluded companies that succeeded in operating at a high level of profitability only did so by branching out into new, uncontested markets. What's more, they fought the competition head on by also staying in highly crowded and contested markets, as mainstream thinkers within the field of strategic management often advocate.

Contribution in Context

Although Kim and Mauborgne implied that their idea was revolutionary, it was in fact not entirely new upon publication. Five years prior to the publication of *Blue Ocean Strategy*, two Swedish authors, Jonas Ridderstråle* and the economist Kjell Nordström,* outlined a similar argument in the book *Funky Business: Talent Makes Capital Dance.*[5] In that book, they urged companies to develop a strategy that changes the game of competition by creating a temporary monopoly* (a situation in which there is only a single supplier of a product or service) in a new market. In 2003, the American marketer Philip Kotler* and the Spanish economist Fernando Trías de Bes* also covered parallel ground in a book called *Lateral Marketing: New Techniques for Finding Breakthrough Ideas.*[6] Kotler and Trías de Bes suggest that companies should not merely create sub-markets within their industry, but actually diverge from the competition through creative development of new consumer needs or usage patterns. This included the energy drink company Red Bull's* solution of developing a soft drink designed primarily to provide energy rather than quench thirst. These and other books[7] published prior to *Blue*

Ocean Strategy urge managers to avoid head-on competition by creating new markets. In this respect, *Blue Ocean Strategy*'s main ideas are nothing new. Its originality lies in its "how to": that is, the book provides a step-by-step guide that explains exactly how companies can create new, uncontested markets.

NOTES

1   Michael E. Porter, *Competitive Strategy: Techniques for Analyzing Industries and Competitors* (New York: Free Press, 1980), 6.

2   *Blue Ocean Strategy*, "A Conversation with W. Chan Kim and Renée Mauborgne," accessed June 20, 2015, http://www.blueoceanstrategy.com/wp-content/uploads/2013/06/AuthorsQandA.pdf.

3   *Blue Ocean Strategy*, "A Conversation with W. Chan Kim and Renée Mauborgne."

4   W. Chan Kim and Renée Mauborgne, "Value Innovation: The Strategic Logic of High Growth," *Harvard Business Review* 75 (1997): 104.

5   Jonas Ridderstråle and Kjell Nordström, *Funky Business: Talent Makes Capital Dance* (Financial Times/Prentice Hall, 2007).

6   Philip Kotler and Fernando Trías de Bes, *Lateral Marketing: New Techniques for Finding Breakthrough Ideas* (Hoboken: John Wiley & Sons, 2003).

7   Ram Charan and Noel M. Tichy, *Every Business is a Growth Business: How Your Company Can Prosper Year After Year* (New York: Random House, 1998); Adrian Slywotzky et al., *How to Grow When Markets Don't* (New York: Warner Business Books, 2003).

SECTION 2
IDEAS

MODULE 5
MAIN IDEAS

KEY POINTS

- *Blue Ocean Strategy* revolves around several analytical frameworks for managers to apply when looking for blue oceans*—markets without competition.*

- The authors argue that companies can find blue ocean markets by creating "value innovation"* and following specified steps to success.

- *Blue Ocean Strategy* is clearly presented and makes significant use of allegory and example.

Key Themes

W. Chan Kim and Renée Mauborgne's *Blue Ocean Strategy* revolves around two thematic concepts—blue oceans and red oceans*—and discusses how managers can use these concepts to avoid or sidestep competition. Beyond these themes, the authors argue that corporate strategists can identify possible blue oceans by applying a sequence of six analytical frameworks.

The process begins with the evaluation of a company's position in terms of major competitive factors in the given industry. The factors identified feed into the second framework, designed to help managers create focus, diverge from the competition, and develop a compelling tagline. As a third step, the authors outline a system that helps conceptually restructure the industry's boundaries; the fourth, in turn, helps develop a business model based on exceptional utility to the customer, strategic pricing and strategic cost. The fifth framework helps managers utilize so-called Hot Spots* (areas in which a small investment of resources can have a significant positive impact), Cold

> **❝** What consistently separated winners from losers
> in creating blue oceans was their approach to strategy.
> The companies caught in the red ocean followed a
> conventional approach, racing to beat the competition
> by building a defensible position within the existing
> industry order. The creators of blue oceans ... followed
> a different strategic logic that we call value innovation. **❞**
>
> W. Chan Kim and Renée Mauborgne, *Blue Ocean Strategy: How to Create
> Uncontested Market Space and Make the Competition Irrelevant*

Spots* (areas which require a large investment) and Horse Trading* (a process of trading excess capacity—when production is less than optimal for a firm—between departments) to harness their company's resources for the greatest impact.[1]

Finally, the authors recommend a paradigm (a conceptual model of how the company could operate) that helps managers gain their employees' trust and ensure their commitment to the process.

Blue Ocean Strategy introduces readers to these themes in a manner that progresses through the book's three parts. The first part introduces the concept, analytical tools, and framework of the book's eponymous strategy; the second part goes into greater depth explaining how to develop a blue ocean strategy. The third and final part describes the execution of the strategy.

Exploring the Ideas

According to Kim and Mauborgne, the "cornerstone of blue ocean strategy" is what they call value innovation. Instead of focusing on "beating the competition," companies practicing value innovation "focus on making the competition irrelevant by creating a leap in value for buyers and your company, thereby opening up new and uncontested market space."[2] An important feature of this framework is that it "defies one of the most commonly accepted dogmas of competition-based strategy: the value-cost trade-off."*[3] Whereas conventional wisdom suggests companies must either create value or lower costs, Kim and Mauborgne argue that businesses can achieve both.

The authors state the first step to establish a blue ocean strategy is to identify the main competitive factors that deserve a company's focus. This can be done by evaluating the company's performance in the industry's most vital areas—price, customer convenience, and environmental sustainability, for example—and comparing it to the competition. Then, companies are advised to select a small number of these areas to focus on as a basis for differentiating* their products. Once these are chosen, companies must identify existing products or product lines for which a minute additional investment could provide exceptional value to a new market.[4] At this point, the blue ocean strategy has been fashioned, and what remains is to execute it by allocating resources to innovating the identified parts of their business.[5]

The authors note that providing the necessary support to employees is a must, and one of the steps to do so, for example, involves integrating the strategy into the company's culture: "You must create a culture of trust and commitment that motivates people to execute the agreed strategy … people's minds and hearts must align with the new strategy."[6] If companies complete these steps, Kim and Mauborgne argue, they can successfully create an uncontested market.[7]

Language and Expression
The ideas in *Blue Ocean Strategy* are structured in a logical, coherent manner, and are intentionally expressed in simple language that non-specialists can easily understand and follow. The most recognizable feature of this accessible style involves their rich use of allegory and example to express the main ideas in their text. The title of the book offers perhaps the best example of this, but there are others. The

authors frequently refer to the story of the Canadian touring circus show Cirque du Soleil* to describe what they mean by a blue ocean: "Cirque du Soleil paid no heed to what the competition did. Instead of following the conventional logic of outpacing the competition by offering a better solution to the given problem—creating a circus with even greater fun and thrills—it sought to offer people the fun and thrill of the circus and the intellectual sophistication and artistic richness of the theatre at the same time."[8]

One important idea lacking deeper analysis in the book involves the possible risk* associated with finding a blue ocean. Risk exists because while company A must invest significant resources to research, develop and create a new and uncontested market, it costs company B very little to observe and analyze company A's experiences in the new market, learn from their mistakes, and then enter that newly created market to dominate it.[9]

Unfortunately, Kim and Mauborgne do not mention any strategies for reducing the amount of risk associated with their approach, which can be thought of as a blue ocean suddenly turning red. Instead, they simply urge the reader to follow the steps and frameworks presented in their book, and assure them that success (as opposed to nimble competitors) will follow.[10]

NOTES

1   Kim W. Chan and Renée Mauborgne, *Blue Ocean Strategy: How to Create Uncontested Market Space and Make the Competition Irrelevant* (Boston: Harvard Business Press, 2005), 156.

2   Kim and Mauborgne, *Blue Ocean Strategy*, 12.

3   Kim and Mauborgne, *Blue Ocean Strategy*, 13.

4   Kim and Mauborgne, *Blue Ocean Strategy*, 13.

5   Kim and Mauborgne, *Blue Ocean Strategy*, 157–61.

6   Kim and Mauborgne, *Blue Ocean Strategy*, 171.

7   Kim and Mauborgne, *Blue Ocean Strategy*, 172–4.

8   Kim and Mauborgne, *Blue Ocean Strategy*, 14.

9   Constantinos C. Markides and Paul A. Geroski, *Fast Second: How Smart Companies Bypass Radical Innovation to Enter and Dominate New Markets* (San Francisco: Jossey-Bass, 2005).

10 Bernard Buisson and Philippe Silberzahn, "Blue Ocean or Fast-second Innovation? A Four-breakthrough Model to Explain Successful Market Domination," *International Journal of Innovation Management* 14 (2010): 359–78.

MODULE 6
SECONDARY IDEAS

KEY POINTS

- Secondary ideas in *Blue Ocean Strategy* include action frameworks designed to lead managers towards the creation of value.*

- Some of these frameworks have been overlooked in the reception of the book yet remain valuable.

- The most useful of the secondary ideas is the "strategy canvas," which highlights the areas in which companies compete.

Other Ideas

The "strategy canvas" and the "Eliminate-Reduce-Raise-Create Grid" represent two of the most important secondary ideas in W. Chan Kim and Renée Mauborgne's *Blue Ocean Strategy*.

With a strategy canvas, managers are asked to compile a list of the most important factors that companies compete over (including price and convenience), and consider what consumers gain from one's own company and from the competitors' companies.[1] This results in a visual representation of a company's relative performance across the factors that define competition* in their industry. These factors then transfer into the Eliminate-Reduce-Raise-Create Grid, a tool that helps managers decide which of the four actions to take and to what degree. This allows a company to differentiate* products from the competition in a way that positions them to serve an entirely new market with a newly designed product.[2]

Based on this redesign of the product's characteristics, a "value curve" is drawn on the strategy canvas to ensure that the company's

> **❝ The strategy canvas is both a diagnostic and an action framework for building a compelling blue ocean strategy. ❞**
> W. Chan Kim and Renée Mauborgne, *Blue Ocean Strategy: How to Create Uncontested Market Space and Make the Competition Irrelevant*

strategy differs from that of the competition. Analysis of this value curve allows the firm to focus on a particular market, diverge from the competition's offerings, and to create a compelling tagline, so creating value for the customer.[3]

Kim and Mauborgne developed these frameworks of value creation* in the 1990s, independently of the book's main argument, through research published in the *Harvard Business Review*.[4] Because they existed separately from *Blue Ocean Strategy*'s larger arguments about new market development,* the possibility exists that even readers who reject the book's broader claims may find the value creation subtext useful and worthwhile.

Exploring the Ideas

In order to guide managers in developing a value curve, Kim and Mauborgne outline what they call the "Four Actions Framework," built around four key questions:

- "Which of the factors that the industry takes for granted should be *eliminated*?"
- "Which factors should be *reduced well below* the industry's standard?"
- "Which factors should be *raised well above* the industry's standard?"
- "Which factors should be *created* that the industry has never offered?"[5]

The italicized words represent the four actions, and the authors approach these questions with examples, as they do with many ideas in *Blue Ocean Strategy*. One such example involves the Australian wine producer Casella Wines. As they write: "In the case of the US wine industry, by thinking in terms of these four actions vis-à-vis the current industry logic and looking across alternatives and non-customers, Casella Wines created [yellow tail],* a wine whose strategic profile broke from the competition and created a blue ocean."*[6]

The innovation Casella made was to create a "social drink accessible to everyone: beer drinkers, cocktail drinkers, and [drinkers of] other non-wine beverages."[7] The Yellow Tail brand, stylized "[yellow tail]," grew rapidly because it was "a completely new combination of wine characteristics that produced an uncomplicated wine structure." That is, those fond of other drinks, and who harbored some skepticism about wine, could appreciate the wine's appeal.[8] Further, the brand limited selection of its product by reducing the range of wines offered and branding each bottle with "bright, vibrant" colors."[9]

Overlooked

Blue Ocean Strategy has garnered attention within the competitive strategy field because it advocates making the competition in an existing market irrelevant by creating new markets absent of any rivals. However, key aspects of the text have received little attention. Arguably the most overlooked component in the book is the series of step-by-step frameworks the authors put forward to help practitioners develop and implement their own strategy of new market creation.

Similarly overlooked is the Pioneer-Migrator-Settler (PMS) Map, one of the most valuable but neglected frameworks offered in the text.[10] A useful market analysis tool, the PMS Map helps managers evaluate the competition in terms of the value they offer. "Pioneers" (according to this framework) offer unprecedented, innovative value; "migrators" provide improved value, and "settlers" put forth the basic "me-too" value (offering the same value within a given product as competitors) that the market demands.

In this framework, the authors attempt to direct managers to the future: "Revenue, profitability, market share, and customer satisfaction are all measures of a company's current position … Chief executives should instead use value and innovation as the important parameters for managing their portfolio of businesses."[11] The objective of managers, the authors argue, should be to "shift the balance of their future portfolio toward pioneers."[12] The PMS Map offers a useful visual representation of this goal that literally allows managers to see the future.

NOTES

1   Kim W. Chan and Renée Mauborgne, *Blue Ocean Strategy: How to Create Uncontested Market Space and Make the Competition Irrelevant* (Boston: Harvard Business Press, 2005), 25.

2   Kim and Mauborgne, *Blue Ocean Strategy*, 35.

3   Kim and Mauborgne, *Blue Ocean Strategy*, 39.

4   W. Chan Kim and Renée Mauborgne, "Value Innovation: The Strategic Logic of High Growth," *Harvard Business Review* 82 (2004): 172–80.

5   Kim and Mauborgne, *Blue Ocean Strategy*, 29.

6   Kim and Mauborgne, *Blue Ocean Strategy*, 31.

7   Kim and Mauborgne, *Blue Ocean Strategy*, 31.

8   Kim and Mauborgne, *Blue Ocean Strategy*, 31.

9   Kim and Mauborgne, *Blue Ocean Strategy*, 33.

10 Kim and Mauborgne, *Blue Ocean Strategy*, 96–8.

11 Kim and Mauborgne, *Blue Ocean Strategy*, 97.

12 Kim and Mauborgne, *Blue Ocean Strategy*, 97.

MODULE 7
ACHIEVEMENT

KEY POINTS

- The authors of *Blue Ocean Strategy* mostly succeeded in achieving their goals.

- The book's achievement is enhanced by the work of others who have confirmed some of the authors' claims through their subsequent work.

- The book fails to accurately capture the risks* involved in carrying out a blue ocean* strategy, marking an important limitation.

Assessing the Argument

W. Chan Kim and Renée Mauborgne had three goals when writing *Blue Ocean Strategy: How to Create Uncontested Market Space and Make the Competition Irrelevant*—and largely succeeded in achieving each. First, they challenged companies to break out of the overcrowded, fiercely contested markets in which they operated, and instead create new markets without peers or competitors.[1] Accordingly, the first part of the book explains the concept of new market development,* outlines its purpose, and highlights the advantages of its application. They accomplish this primarily through the metaphor of the red ocean* (a crowded, highly competitive market metaphorically stained with the blood of intense zero-sum* competition,* in which one company's gain is another's loss) and the blue ocean (a brand-new market free of rivals).

The authors are not satisfied with merely convincing readers of the blue ocean strategy's merits, however; they also seek to make it as easy as possible for practitioners to put this approach to use in their

> 66 How are you pursuing the next big thing? Stay connected with your clients and continue to listen to what they want and learn how to better serve them through innovation. Discover a blue ocean and you will make the competition irrelevant. 99
>
> Les Kollegian,* CEO of the design and branding agency Jacob Tyler

organizations. In fact, Kim and Mauborgne endeavor to make it just as simple for practitioners to form and execute a blue ocean strategy as to pursue the kind of competition-based strategy that most would probably find more familiar and comfortable. To that end, the second part of the book devotes itself to presenting several practical frameworks in great detail. One step at a time, each framework takes managers through the process of developing and executing a blue ocean strategy that works for their specific organization and industry.

Finally, the authors intended their work to break free from the mainstream view commonly held in strategic management. This traditional view focuses on developing strategic tools that support managers in competing head on with the competition—which they have no choice but to confront in a crowded market with rigid, unchangeable boundaries. And because Kim and Mauborgne run counter in their approach to these widely accepted assumptions about how markets work, readers may need to keep an open mind in order to fully grasp and appreciate the authors' intention in this regard.[2] They also caution that the same counterintuitive strokes that make the text potentially challenging can also present obstacles for practitioners who seek to implement blue ocean ideas in their organizations. For that reason, Kim and Mauborgne give the topic of overcoming organizational hurdles[3] careful attention in the third part of the book, paying particular attention to the importance of fairness in the process of winning over people's trust and fair incentives.

Achievement in Context

As prominent business scholars, Kim and Mauborgne enjoyed all the benefits of association with a major university—the business school INSEAD* in Fontainebleau, France—and thus faced few restrictions, either financial or intellectual, in writing *Blue Ocean Strategy*. Further, the authors had time to develop their ideas over several years, and in multiple articles published in prominent business publications such as the *Harvard Business Review*. Still, their ideas emanate from a specific set of business cases and should be viewed in that context.

A small number of researchers have attempted to probe how the concepts in *Blue Ocean Strategy* apply to contexts beyond those referenced in their book. And so far, their findings indicate that the book's conclusions may have a wider relevance than critics realize.[4] For example, even though the concepts in *Blue Ocean Strategy* were designed for use at the top level of a firm, some researchers have tested whether its framework could be successfully deployed in just a single division of a company.[5] As *Blue Ocean Strategy* promises comparatively high profits,* a team of researchers put this premise to the test in 2011. Led by Petri Parvinen* (a visiting scholar at Stanford University and a professor at the Helsinki School of Economics), they decided on a litmus test—a test designed to give a decisive answer—for success: could a blue ocean approach increase a division's financial performance? Ultimately, they found that Kim and Mauborgne's ideas could indeed be applied to a business's sales department, for example, and achieve high profit increases. This and other studies would seem to indicate that the concepts in *Blue Ocean Strategy* do apply in different contexts.

Limitations

The argument in *Blue Ocean Strategy* specifically applies only to companies in low-growth industries—and this constitutes the framework's greatest limitation. Companies situated in a shifting, growing market would be ill- advised to take on the high risk involved in creating a new market. Likewise, companies with scarce resources (such as high-tech, entrepreneurial ventures in their first stages of growth), or firms capable of consistently outperforming the competition, should avoid the risk of trying to develop and succeed in a new market. And so, given the prospects of failure entailed in creating a new market, *Blue Ocean Strategy* has limited applicability in situations dominated by fierce competitive rivalry and low market growth.

Yet, unfortunately, Kim and Mauborgne have a less conservative estimation of the risks and limitations their ideas present—and forcefully advocate for new market creation as a general cure-all for lagging profitability. This becomes problematic given *Blue Ocean Strategy*'s appeal to a non-scholarly audience of business managers. While scholars will know of the body of literature from the 1980s[6] that reveals the limitations in Kim and Mauborgne's core argument, most professional managers will not approach the book with this important caveat in mind. As a consequence, it is worrisome that Kim and Mauborgne do not explore the potential uncertainties involved in their proposal; they suggest frameworks offered in their book are a viable path to success.[7] The precarious risks that come with creating a new market can cripple a company due to substantial losses. That the authors fail to acknowledge such risks represents a potentially serious omission. Readers unfamiliar with the wider literature on this topic, who implement the ideas without weighing the dangers, could unintentionally cause their companies to bleed—creating a red ocean of another kind.

NOTES

1   Kim W. Chan and Renée Mauborgne, *Blue Ocean Strategy: How to Create Uncontested Market Space and Make the Competition Irrelevant* (Boston: Harvard Business Press, 2005), 4.

2   Kim and Mauborgne, *Blue Ocean Strategy*, 4.

3   Kim and Mauborgne, *Blue Ocean Strategy*, 147–8.

4   Emiel F. M. Wubben et al., "Finding Uncontested Markets for European Fruit and Vegetables Through Applying the Blue Ocean Strategy," *British Food Journal* 114 (2012): 248–71; Jen-te Yang, "Identifying the Attributes of Blue Ocean Strategy in Hospitality," *International Journal of Contemporary Hospitality Management* 24 (2012): 701–20; Dennis Pitta, "Issues in a Down Economy: Blue Oceans and New Product Development," *Journal of Product and Brand Management* 18 (2009): 292–6.

5   Petri Parvinen et al., "Awareness, Action and Context-specificity of Blue Ocean Practices in Sales Management," *Management Decision* 49 (2011): 1218–34.

6   Bernard Buisson and Philippe Silberzahn, "Blue Ocean or Fast-second Innovation? A Four-breakthrough Model to Explain Successful Market Domination," *International Journal of Innovation Management* 14 (2010): 359–78.

7   Buisson and Silberzahn, "Blue Ocean or Fast-second Innovation? A Four-breakthrough Model to Explain Successful Market Domination," 364.

MODULE 8
PLACE IN THE AUTHOR'S WORK

KEY POINTS

- *Blue Ocean Strategy* in many ways represents the intellectual and professional culmination of both authors' work.

- The book builds on a series of articles published in the Harvard Business Review as well as other academic papers.

- *Blue Ocean Strategy* remains a significant work in the business world; it is almost certainly the most important contribution Kim and Mauborgne have made to the field.

Positioning

Blue Ocean Strategy: How to Create Uncontested Market Space and Make the Competition Irrelevant represents the culmination of more than 15 years of research by W. Chan Kim and Renée Mauborgne on topics pertinent to the field of strategy and management; these include value innovation,[*][1] creating new market space[2] (identifying new territories for companies to enter where they may add value systematically across competitive markets, rather than competing head-to-head in a given sector), and fair process[3] (a management tool for companies transitioning from a production-based to knowledge-based economy in which value creation[*] depends on an innovation of ideas). Initial presentations of these results were published in a series of academic journal articles, mostly in the prestigious *Harvard Business Review*. In their 1999 article "Creating New Market Space," the authors introduced their groundbreaking ideas: "Most companies focus on matching and beating their rivals, and as a result their strategies tend to converge along the same basic dimensions of competition ... As rivals outdo one another, they end up competing solely on the basis of

> **❝** The contents of this book are based on more than fifteen years of research, data stretching back more than a hundred years, and a series of Harvard Business Review articles as well as academic articles on various dimensions of this topic. The ideas, tools, and frameworks presented here have been further tested and refined over the years in corporate practice in Europe, the United States, and Asia. **❞**
>
> W. Chan Kim and Renée Mauborgne, *Blue Ocean Strategy: How to Create Uncontested Market Space and Make the Competition Irrelevant*

incremental improvements in cost or quality or both."[4]

In other words, this convergence of competition leads to the value-cost trade-off* that underlies *Blue Ocean Strategy*.

Published in 2005, *Blue Ocean Strategy* distills the authors' findings from this period of research. This book constitutes their most important contribution to the field of business strategy* to date, and has provided the jumping-off point for the authors' careers in the years since.

This popular book is widely read in business literature circles. In 2007 Kim and Mauborgne established the Blue Ocean Strategy Institute* at their home institution, the French campus of the business school INSEAD.* The Institute's mission is to promote the book's ideas in academia and the practical business world,[5] by fostering research based on the book's analysis and offering courses pegged to the book's concepts.

Integration

All of this began with a progressive trajectory that progressed from Kim and Mauborgne's research, to the publication of *Blue Ocean Strategy*, to their current work at the Blue Ocean Strategy Institute.

This steady growth in scope and influence, which has lasted more than a decade after the book's publication, indicates that Kim and Mauborgne's ideas have remained unified and coherent—and there have been no significant modifications on their conclusions to date. Even so, as of 2015 both authors remain active in their profession, so it may be premature to conclude that they will not augment their key ideas in the future.

Additionally, the authors have published little work on topics unrelated to blue oceans;* the bulk of their academic output since 2005 has sought to expand and promote the ideas in *Blue Ocean Strategy*. In their 2015 article "Red Ocean Traps," for example, the authors describe the "traps" businesses face in today's sluggish economy by using the red ocean/* blue ocean framework: "In the decade since the publication of the first edition of our book, *Blue Ocean Strategy*, we've had conversations with many managers involved in executing market-creating strategies. As they shared their successes and failures with us, we identified a common factor that seemed to consistently undermine their efforts: their mental models." Many of these "mental models" relate to the conventional wisdom of red oceans. For example, the authors argue that companies suffer when they assume that market creation involves a trade-off between value and cost. As they write: "A market-creating move is a 'both-and,' not an 'either-or,' strategy." [6]

Significance

On the whole, it is fair to say that, at this point of their careers, Kim and Mauborgne have made notable contributions to the field of strategic management. While their journal articles in the *Harvard Business Review* received wide attention in the scholarly community, *Blue Ocean Strategy* has elevated them to something of a celebrity status among mainstream business practitioners. Since its publication, *Blue Ocean Strategy* has topped numerous best seller lists around the world, won several awards, and been translated into 43 languages; some observers consider it one of the most successful business books ever written. The book has been referenced in passing in more than 1,000 articles, and several studies have tested the applicability of Kim and Mauborgne's ideas beyond the markets the authors studied. So far, however, no particular school of thinkers has coalesced around this text.

With this in mind, it is fair to argue that the best measure of Kim and Mauborgne's contribution is the book's use in the business world. To some extent this is difficult to quantify. But endorsements from business leaders indicate that their work has been notably influential.

NOTES

1 W. Chan Kim and Renée Mauborgne, "Value Innovation: The Strategic Logic of High Growth," *Harvard Business Review* 75 (1997): 103–12.

2 W. Chan Kim and Renée Mauborgne, "Creating New Market Space," *Harvard Business Review* 77 (1999): 83–93.

3 W. Chan Kim and Renée Mauborgne, "Fair Process: Managing in the Knowledge Economy," *Harvard Business Review* 75 (1997): 65–75.

4 Kim and Mauborgne, "Creating New Market Space," 83.

5 Satheesh Kumar, "Blue Ocean Strategy: How to Create Uncontested Market Space and Make the Competition Irrelevant," *South Asian Journal of Management* 15 (2008): 121–4.

6 W. Chan Kim and Renée Mauborgne, "Red Ocean Traps," *Harvard Business Review*, accessed June 18, 2015, https://hbr.org/2015/03/red-ocean-traps.

SECTION 3
IMPACT

MODULE 9
THE FIRST RESPONSES

KEY POINTS

- Critics of *Blue Ocean Strategy* pointed out that the book was not original, ignored the important idea of "second-mover advantage,"* and overlooked the concept of risk.*

- Although the authors did not respond directly to critics, they did modify their position slightly to allow for multiple approaches to strategy.

- The book will likely be seen as one approach to strategy among many, rather than a unified strategic-thinking model.

Criticism

W. Chan Kim and Renée Mauborgne's main argument in *Blue Ocean Strategy: How to Create Uncontested Market Space and Make the Competition Irrelevant*—that managers should create uncontested markets to "make the competition irrelevant"[1]—spurred several important critiques following its 2005 publication. These centered on the book's lack of originality; the inaccuracy of its claims; its failure to point out well-known risks connected to the solution it proposes; and its omission of well-documented alternatives.

The first criticism, articulated by the business scholars Bernard Buisson* and Philippe Silberzahn,* asserts that the book merely repackages old ideas put forth by other authors.[2] Indeed, *Blue Ocean Strategy's* main argument appears to merely restate what those in business studies commonly refer to as "first-mover advantage"* (the advantage conferred on the first company to move into a particular market, particularly with regard to resources). Several popular business books advocated first-mover advantage before *Blue Ocean Strategy* was

> ❝ Innovation can be simple and rely on only one breakthrough ... In most cases of market domination, however, the successful innovation relies on a combination of breakthroughs. ❞
>
> Bernard Buisson and Philippe Silberzahn, "Blue Ocean or Fast-second Innovation?"

published in 2005.[3] In 2003's *How to Grow When Markets Don't*, the American economic theorist Adrian Slywotzky* and his co-authors argue that "demand innovation," or "creating *new growth* by expanding the market's boundaries," is key to expanding a business when markets dry up.[4] Demand innovation theory (the need for increased entrepreneurship to meet high-sector demands in society) closely parallels Kim and Mauborgne's blue ocean* model.

Further, Buisson and Silberzahn criticize the authors' failure to mention what is known as "second-mover advantage."* Once "first movers" pioneer a new market—and that market begins to sprout— "second movers" with considerable financial resources will move to dominate that new market and reap the spoils of its growth.[5] As Buisson and Silberzahn write: "It is not necessary to create a market to end up dominating it. Google,* today's leading Internet search engine, was a late entrant to the market, coming a good two years after pioneer AltaVista."*[6] (Countless other examples exist: Google also came after Yahoo!* and toppled it from dominance; the first handheld MP3* player came well before Apple's* iPod.) They go on to say that "almost any differentiated product* can be cast ex post as a blue ocean strategy."[7]

A final important critique of *Blue Ocean Strategy* focused on how it neglected the topic of risk and hazard in business. Despite the high failure rate demonstrated among other companies seeking a "first-mover advantage,"[8] Kim and Mauborgne neglect to mention any strategies for reducing the risk their approach assumes. Instead, they suggest the tools they provide in their book's framework as a path to success.[9]

Responses

Since the 2005 publication of *Blue Ocean Strategy* Kim and Mauborgne have written just one journal article, in 2009.[10] In it, they continued to champion the *Blue Ocean Strategy* paradigm, insisting that companies should develop new markets to "make competition irrelevant"[11]— and realize unprecedented profit* growth as a result. In their steadfast support of their original argument, the authors failed to meaningfully engage the substantial critiques of *Blue Ocean Strategy*.

Still there has been one detectable (if slight) change in Kim and Mauborgne's stance: a softened tone toward mainstream strategic theory that focuses on fighting the competition rather than creating new markets. In *Blue Ocean Strategy* they rejected this position and depicted their own strategy as a superior alternative—but in 2009 they admitted that in some cases, a competitive approach could be justified. As they write: "When the structural conditions of an industry or environment are attractive and you have the resources and capabilities to carve out a viable competitive position, the structuralist* approach is likely to produce good returns."[12]

Further, they argue that this approach is appropriate and justifiable when a company has the proper resources and capabilities to perform well in a certain market environment, is already beating the competition, or is too risk-averse to create a new market. In particular, the last point deserves attention: it is the most acknowledgement Kim and Mauborgne have given to the high amount of risk involved in new market creation, which forms the cornerstone of their proposed strategy.

Conflict and Consensus

Because of Kim and Mauborgne's failure to answer their critics' arguments, the two sides have not yet reached a consensus. However, it seems a positive step that the authors have expressed more tolerance towards mainstream literature on strategy theory. Specifically, they have embraced the possibility that alternative approaches to strategy will be more effective in many cases—and that only a limited set of companies might have the means and determination to scout out blue oceans.

The consensus view of the text will likely conclude that a blue ocean strategy will be a good fit for some companies, but not applicable in all cases. As analysts associated with the consulting firm A. T. Kearney* note, *Blue Ocean Strategy* is part of a group of "useful ideas" that mirror the "best practices of successful companies."[13] And so many analysts have adopted this view of the book: a good idea but not offering a unified approach to strategy. In other words, analyses such as *Blue Ocean Strategy* equal "recipes for slicing the strategic pie rather than creating the overall strategic frameworks borne of the strategy heydays."[14]

Conclusions such as this refer to a period ending in the 1990s when strategy theory sought comprehensive models—and set certain measures of completeness that *Blue Ocean Strategy* does not quite meet.

NOTES

1   Kim W. Chan and Renée Mauborgne, *Blue Ocean Strategy: How to Create Uncontested Market Space and Make the Competition Irrelevant* (Boston: Harvard Business Press, 2005), 5.

2   Bernard Buisson and Philippe Silberzahn, "Blue Ocean or Fast-second Innovation? A Four-breakthrough Model to Explain Successful Market Domination," *International Journal of Innovation Management* 14 (2010): 359–78.

3   Jonas Ridderstråle and Kjell Nordström, *Funky Business: Talent Makes Capital Dance* (Financial Times/Prentice Hall, 2007); Ram Charan and Noel M. Tichy, *Every Business is a Growth Business: How Your Company Can Prosper Year After Year* (New York: Random House, 1998); Philip Kotler and Fernando Trías de Bes, *Lateral Marketing: New Techniques for Finding Breakthrough Ideas* (Hoboken: John Wiley & Sons, 2003); Adrian Slywotzky et al., *How to Grow When Markets Don't* (New York: Warner Business Books, 2003).

4   Slywotzky et al., *How to Grow When Markets Don't.*

5   Buisson and Silberzahn, "Blue Ocean or Fast-second Innovation?" 360.

6   Buisson and Silberzahn, "Blue Ocean or Fast-second Innovation?" 363.

7   Buisson and Silberzahn, "Blue Ocean or Fast-second Innovation?" 364.

8   Peter N. Golder and Gerard J. Tellis, "Pioneer Advantage: Marketing Logic or MarketingLegend?" *Journal of Marketing Research* 30 (1993): 158–70.

9   Buisson and Silberzahn, "Blue Ocean or Fast-second Innovation?" 360.

10 W. Chan Kim and Renée Mauborgne, "How Strategy Shapes Structure," *Harvard Business Review* 87 (2009): 72–80.

11 Kim and Mauborgne, "How Strategy Shapes Structure," 72–80.

12 Kim and Mauborgne, "How Strategy Shapes Structure," 74.

13 Johan Aurik et al., "The History of Strategy and its Future Prospects," 9, *A.T. Kearney,* accessed June 15, 2015, https://www.atkearney.com/ documents/10192/4260571/History+of+Strategy+and+Its+Future +Prospects.pdf/29f8c6e8-7cdb-4a25-8acc-b0c39e4439e1

14 Aurik et al., "The History of Strategy and its Future Prospects," 9.

MODULE 10
THE EVOLVING DEBATE

KEY POINTS

- *Blue Ocean Strategy* has helped focus attention on creating new markets, and shifted intellectual energy in that direction.

- The text has not produced a defined school of thought, though a number of practitioners have adopted its ideas.

- The book's limited importance among academics is perhaps related to its popularity in the business community, where it is widely read and applied.

Uses and Problems

W. Chan Kim and Renée Mauborgne's *Blue Ocean Strategy: How to Create Uncontested Market Space and Make the Competition Irrelevant* was not the first work to propose new market creation as an alternative to head-on competition*[1]—but it has revitalized interest in the idea by providing practitioners and theorists alike with user-friendly tools for creating new markets. And this is where its key value lies, because these frameworks have made a true contribution to the field of strategy. This is reflected in how contemporary strategy specialists have begun to adopt Kim and Mauborgne's frameworks in their own research, and apply them to business contexts other than the ones Kim and Mauborgne examined in their work.[2] As a result, the concept of a "blue ocean"* has entered the business vernacular.

Despite the book's popularity, its influence should not negate the value of those traditional ways of understanding business and markets oriented towards competition. Kim and Mauborgne acknowledge that their ideas on new market creation can never replace conventional, competition–oriented strategic theories. Rather, they see them as

> ❝ Although it was written with big corporate executives in mind, I don't think enough entrepreneurs have read *Blue Ocean Strategy*. The basic proposition? Create a 'blue ocean' of uncontested market space, and avoid the shark-infested 'red ocean' of intense competition. ❞
>
> Rob Coneybeer, founder of Shasta Ventures

complementary because of a time-honored business cycle: as soon as competitors move in to challenge one's position in a newly created market, competitive strategic moves become relevant again. Put another way, blue oceans do not stay blue indefinitely. Regardless, Kim and Mauborgne's *Blue Ocean Strategy*, while it does not represent a proverbial sea change in contemporary strategic thinking, nevertheless makes an important contribution.

Schools of Thought

More than 1,000 academic journal articles cite *Blue Ocean Strategy*, with some exploring the validity of Kim and Mauborgne's ideas in sectors not mentioned in the text, such as the hospitality[3] and banking industries,[4] as well as in international markets.[5] While most researchers have applied the concepts of *Blue Ocean Strategy* to corporate strategy—as was intended by Kim and Mauborgne[6]—others have examined the applications in specific divisions. With sales departments, for example, researchers have concluded that the framework can in fact produce benefits.[7]

Besides academics, practitioners have also come to value Kim and Mauborgne's concepts.[8] This is not entirely by accident: In 2007 the authors established the Blue Ocean Strategy Institute* to advance their ideas both in academia and the practical business world.[9] The institute does this by promoting research, based on the book's analyses, in the corporate, public, and social sectors; it also offers courses to students and managers that examine the book's concepts.[10]

Despite the relatively wide acceptance of *Blue Ocean Strategy,* no identifiable school of thought has formed around the text. One possible reason might involve the resemblance of the book's main ideas to those of other authors published in earlier texts.[11] Like Kim and Mauborgne's approach, these similar, earlier frameworks proposed that the development of new markets would create value and growth.

In Current Scholarship

Though widely read by business managers and practitioners, *Blue Ocean Strategy* has been somewhat ignored by scholars. According to some researchers,[12] the book's popularity among non-academics could well explain the paucity of scholarly attention it has received thus far—as scholars are often skeptical of books addressed primarily to a lay audience. Additionally, *Blue Ocean Strategy* has perhaps not yet received nearly as much attention in academia because, for scholars, the idea of creating new markets to "make the competition irrelevant"[13] is not new. Popular concepts such as the "first-mover advantage," and influential books such as *How to Grow When Markets Don't,*[14] co-authored by the economic theorist Adrian Slywotzky,* existed and were studied prior to when Kim and Mauborgne published their approach in book form.

Furthermore, academic studies show that creating a new market is highly risky as strategic moves go. In many cases, the "first mover" into a market loses its edge to companies with more capital that follow it in, and in the process learn from the mistakes that the first mover made.[15] Because both the advantages and disadvantages of first-mover status are well known to academics, the ideas put forward in *Blue Ocean Strategy* may attract little interest among scholarly readers.

NOTES

1   Ram Charan and Noel M. Tichy, *Every Business is a Growth Business: How Your Company Can Prosper Year After Year* (New York: Random House, 1998); Adrian Slywotzky et al., *How to Grow When Markets Don't* (New York: Warner Business Books, 2003).

2   Emiel F.M. Wubben et al., "Finding Uncontested Markets for European Fruit and Vegetables Through Applying the Blue Ocean Strategy," *British Food Journal* 114 (2012): 248–71; Jen-te Yang, "Identifying the Attributes of Blue Ocean Strategy in Hospitality," *International Journal of Contemporary Hospitality Management* (2012): 701–20; Dennis Pitta, "Issues in a Down Economy: Blue Oceans and New Product Development," *Journal of Product and Brand Management* 18 (2009): 292–6.

3   Yang, "Identifying the Attributes of Blue Ocean Strategy in Hospitality."

4   Daewoo Park et al., "Effects of Market Boundaries and Market Competition on Business Strategy in the United States Banking Sector," *International Journal of Management* 28 (2011): 363–8.

5   Andrejs Čirjevskis et al., "New Approaches in Measuring and Assessing Viability of Blue Ocean Strategy in B2B Sector," *Journal of Business Management* 3 (2010): 162–79.

6   Wubben et al., "Finding Uncontested Markets for European Fruit and Vegetables Through Applying the Blue Ocean Strategy"; Yang, "Identifying the Attributes of Blue Ocean Strategy in Hospitality"; Pitta, "Issues in a Down Economy: Blue Oceans and New Product Development."

7   Petri Parvinen et al., "Awareness, Action and Context-specificity of Blue Ocean Practices in Sales Management," *Management Decision* 49 (2011): 1218–34.

8   Sarah Layton, "Blue Ocean Strategy: How to Create Uncontested Market Space and Make the Competition Irrelevant," *Consulting to Management Magazine* 16 (2005): 57–9.

9   INSEAD business school, "Blue Ocean Strategy Institute," accessed October 30, 2013, http://knowledge.insead.edu/strategy/inseads-global-thought-leaders-w-chan-kim-and-renee-mauborgne-2938.

10 INSEAD business school, "Blue Ocean Strategy Courses," accessed October 29, 2013, http://www.insead.edu/blueoceanstrategyinstitute/MBA/courses.cfm.

11 Charan and Tichy, *Every Business is a Growth Business: How Your Company Can Prosper Year After Year*; Jonas Ridderstråle and Kjell Nordström, *Funky Business: Talent Makes Capital Dance* (Financial Times/Prentice Hall, 2007); Philip Kotler and Fernando Trías de Bes, *Lateral Marketing: New Techniques for Finding Breakthrough Ideas* (Hoboken: John Wiley & Sons, 2003); Slywotzky et al., *How to Grow When Markets Don't*.

12 Parvinen et al., "Awareness, Action and Context-specificity."

13 Kim W. Chan and Renée Mauborgne, *Blue Ocean Strategy: How to Create Uncontested Market Space and Make the Competition Irrelevant* (Boston: Harvard Business Press, 2005), 5.

14 Slywotzky et al., *How to Grow When Markets Don't.*

15 Constantinos C. Markides and Paul A. Geroski, *Fast Second: How Smart Companies Bypass Radical Innovation to Enter and Dominate New Markets* (San Francisco: Jossey-Bass, 2005).

MODULE 11
IMPACT AND INFLUENCE TODAY

KEY POINTS

- *Blue Ocean Strategy* is widely read among business practitioners, particularly those looking to differentiate their product.

- *Blue Ocean Strategy* challenges the traditional strategy frameworks that focus on beating the competition.

- Scholars have tested the ideas in *Blue Ocean Strategy* by applying them in new industries and sectors.

Position

W. Chan Kim and Renée Mauborgne's *Blue Ocean Strategy: How to Create Uncontested Market Space and Make the Competition Irrelevant* remains an important book within the field of business strategy.* The argument that the authors put forth—namely, that firms can increase profits* by creating a new market—has created great enthusiasm among business practitioners, though academics have greeted it more coolly. But a third audience comes into play here: entrepreneurs, including those in the powerful high-tech sector. This is compelling evidence of the book's influence, given that Chan and Mauborgne originally (and exclusively) sought an audience among executives at big corporations.

Some of the entrepreneurial fans of *Blue Ocean Strategy* include the American science writer Tim Ferriss,* an entrepreneur who recommended the book as a guide for companies to differentiate* their product,[1] and Aaron Levie,* CEO of the digital services company Box* who reportedly keeps copies of the book in his office to give his visitors.[2] Echoing a key theme of *Blue Ocean Strategy*, Ferriss

> **66** I really like some of the concepts and frameworks offered by Kim and Mauborgne in their best-selling book, *Blue Ocean Strategy*. However, I think they do a disservice to themselves by positioning their framework against Michael Porter's classic work on strategy. To me, they set up a straw man for the purpose of making their argument more interesting and provocative, but it's not an accurate depiction of Porter's ideas. **99**
>
> Michael Roberto, *Curves: Not Such a Blue Ocean After All*

writes: "If you're aiming to differentiate your company, particularly if you're in a crowded space, you can't just stand to be [the] cheapest as a small company."[3] Similarly, Brian Halligan* of the software company HubSpot* says: "When we first started HubSpot, [we] used *Blue Ocean Strategy* to map out our approach. The book is great at challenging you to differentiate from not only your competitors, but your alternatives."[4] The venture capitalist* Rob Coneybeer,* who encourages start-up founders to read *Blue Ocean Strategy*, has argued that too many entrepreneurs attempt to enter highly competitive markets: "Plenty of people will say '…don't worry about the competition. Just focus on execution.' But don't take that advice to decide where to start a company. Pick an area where there's huge latent demand and no one addressing that need."[5]

Interaction

Blue Ocean Strategy challenges the conventional line of strategic thinking that pushes for fighting the competition* head on. This mainstream approach is exemplified in the work of the strategy scholars Michael Porter* and Jorge Vasconcellos e Sá,* who developed a number of strategies to directly attack and defend against competition.

Despite this challenge, it is reasonable that *Blue Ocean Strategy* can inhabit the same intellectual space as traditional approaches to competition; some business cases call for a blue ocean* approach while others require more traditional methods. Yet is a blue ocean paradigm complementary or contradictory?

Referencing Kim and Mauborgne's example of the American aviation company Southwest Airlines* as a blue ocean company, the management scholar Michael Roberto* offers a pertinent critique of both their approach and the apparently incompatible strategy of the business scholar Michael Porter. "Southwest Airlines created a blue ocean," Kim and Mauborgne write, "by breaking the trade-offs customers had to make between the speed of airplanes and the economy and flexibility of car transport."[6] To do this, the company "pioneered point-to-point [direct] travel between midsize cities; previously, the industry operated through hub-and-spoke systems [whereby local airports offer flights to a central airport for onward travel]."[7]

But Roberto mounts a spirited challenge to this perspective: "How can one possibly argue that [Southwest Airlines is] an example of a firm that has achieved both low cost and differentiation?"[8] Southwest Airlines, he writes, does not embody a product differentiator as Michael Porter would understand it—charging a "price premium" (setting a high price for a product as a means of making the product artificially more appealing), it is simply a "low-cost competitor"[9] (when a company offers a low price for a product in order to stimulate demand in an economy, oftentimes resulting in a competitor's advantage).

The company did not, then, subvert traditional strategy techniques, Roberto concludes; it merely found a way to offer a cheaper product.

The Continuing Debate

Blue Ocean Strategy is now included in the core curriculum in many business schools, and continues to rank among the top best-selling business books of all time.[10] Strategy researchers continue to test the validity of the book's analysis by applying it to business contexts that diverge from those examined by Kim and Mauborgne. Consequently, marketing scholars have found the text's conclusions relevant to business contexts as varied as hospitality[11] and banking,[12] and in domestic and international markets alike.[13] For example, in the paper "New Approaches in Measuring and Assessing Viability of Blue Ocean Strategy in B2B Sector," Andrejs Čirjevskis* of the Riga International School of Economics and Business Administration and his co-authors sought to determine whether blue ocean techniques apply to construction chemical suppliers in Switzerland, and purification equipment manufacturers in Russia. They later confirmed their findings focusing their research on the "strategic move," or the set of actions managers must carry out to create new market space—a concept at the core of *Blue Ocean Strategy*.

Even as the frameworks in *Blue Ocean Strategy* have practical use within the field of strategy, and in business more generally, other fields have by and large ignored the book entirely. And because its usefulness has been limited to a select audience—strategists in large corporations and to some extent entrepreneurs—some have gone so far as to question whether Kim and Mauborgne's ideas have any relevance within the public and non-profit sectors.[14] Yet it is also fair to ask whether any organizations in those areas have put a blue ocean strategy to the test. At this time, this does not seem to be the case, though as the public and non-profit sectors continue to innovate, this gap allows for more possibilities and new testing grounds.

NOTES

1 "Tim Ferriss Answers Your Questions," *Huffington Post*, accessed June 18, 2015, http://www.huffingtonpost.com/shopify/tim-ferriss-answers-your_b_4808715.html.

2 "The Way I Work: Aaron Levie, Box," accessed June 18, 2015, http://www.inc.com/magazine/201211/reshma-memon-yaqub/the-way-i-work-aaron-levie-box.html.

3   "Tim Ferriss Answers Your Questions."

4   Dennis Keohane, "7 Books that Influenced Boston Entrepreneurs and
    Innovators," accessed June 18, 2015, http://venturefizz.com/blog/
    7-books-influenced-boston-entrepreuneurs-and-innovators?utm_source
    =feedburner&utm_medium=feed&utm_campaign=Feed%3A+Venturefizz
    RssFeed+(VentureFizz+RSS+Feed) last accessed June 18, 2015.

5   Rob Coneybeer, "Crowded Markets," accessed June 19, 2015, http://280.
    vc/post/114469065379/crowded-markets.

6   Kim W. Chan and Renée Mauborgne, *Blue Ocean Strategy: How to Create
    Uncontested Market Space and Make the Competition Irrelevant* (Boston:
    Harvard Business Press, 2005), 38.

7   Kim and Mauborgne, *Blue Ocean Strategy*, 39.

8   Michael Roberto, "Curves: Not Such a Blue Ocean After All," accessed June
    19, 2015, http://michael-roberto.blogspot.com/2010/07/curves-not-such-
    blue-ocean-after-all.html.

9   Roberto, "Curves," accessed June 18, 2015.

10 Satheesh Kumar, "Blue Ocean Strategy: How to Create Uncontested Market
    Space and Make the Competition Irrelevant," *South Asian Journal of
    Management* 15 (2008): 121–4.

11 Jen-te Yang, "Identifying the Attributes of Blue Ocean Strategy in
    Hospitality," *International Journal of Contemporary Hospitality Management*
    (2012): 701–20.

12 Daewoo Park et al., "Effects of Market Boundaries and Market Competition
    on Business Strategy in the United States Banking Sector," *International
    Journal of Management* 28 (2011): 363–8.

13 Andrejs Čirjevskis et al., "New Approaches in Measuring and Assessing
    Viability of Blue Ocean Strategy in B2B Sector," *Journal of Business
    Management* 3 (2010): 162–79.

14 Petri Parvinen et al., "Awareness, Action and Context-specificity of Blue
    Ocean Practices in Sales Management," *Management Decision* 49 (2011):
    1218–34.

MODULE 12
WHERE NEXT?

KEY POINTS

- Although the influence of *Blue Ocean Strategy* may fade, the "new market development"* thesis remains an area of active debate.

- The book will continue to have an influence through teaching and analysis founded on its models; Lean LaunchPad,* an entrepreneurial class that began at the University of California at Berkeley, offers an example.

- The book is highly valuable for business and non-business students alike, as it will prepare them for thinking about differentiation* and growth in a highly dynamic economy.

Potential

The central question addressed by W. Chan Kim and Renée Mauborgne's *Blue Ocean Strategy: How to Create Uncontested Market Space and Make the Competition Irrelevant*—how to deal with competition* in a saturated market*—is probably as old as capitalism* (the social and economic model dominant in the West, and increasingly throughout the developing world) itself. The solution the authors propose—that companies can sidestep their competitors by offering innovative value to consumers whose needs have not been addressed—similarly pre-dates *Blue Ocean Strategy*.

Many earlier thinkers[1] proposed very similar strategies to the ones described in Kim and Mauborgne's work. The sheer number of earlier authors who covered this topic highlights it as a recurring theme in strategic thinking. Every few years, a newly minted version of the "new market development" thesis emerges within business literature

> **❝** The six principles of blue ocean strategy proposed in this book should serve as essential pointers for every company thinking about its future strategy if it aspires to lead the increasingly crowded business world ... What we suggest is that to obtain high performance in this overcrowded market, companies should go beyond competing for share to creating blue oceans. **❞**
>
> W. Chan Kim and Renée Mauborgne, *Blue Ocean Strategy: How to Create Uncontested Market Space and Make the Competition Irrelevant*

and catches influential leaders' attention—at least for a short time, until interest fades. And once the memory of that theory or framework dissipates, newer versions pop up and reignite the initial interest. Given that it recycles some previous ideas—though authoritatively so—*Blue Ocean Strategy* could find its success short-lived should a new tome update and repurpose its key points.

However, another possibility exists. Numerous business publications indicate some genuine interest in the "new market development" thesis, and Kim and Mauborgne's version could stand as the one that solved the problem of escaping fierce, head-to-head competition.

There are other good reasons to believe that *Blue Ocean Strategy* will enjoy long-lasting relevance. The novel, detailed and practical frameworks the authors developed as they researched their book have helped firms to assess and restructure their current market position. This prepares managers to redesign their industry's boundaries—a triumphant culmination that constitutes the book's real and possibly lasting contribution to the field of strategy. These tools indicate that the authors thought about their audience as much as they did the soundness of their framework. The idea of new market development as an alternative to fighting competition in a crowded market is thought provoking. But offering a road map to formulate and execute such a strategy is game changing.

Future Directions

One development in business-strategy thinking represents an offshoot to *Blue Ocean Strategy*: the "Lean LaunchPad" concept developed by the American entrepreneur and academic Steve Blank.*[2] Unlike *Blue Ocean Strategy*, which was originally intended for managers in large corporations, the Lean LaunchPad targets start-ups and has gained prominence as a tool that teaches entrepreneurship to students from diverse backgrounds. Blank has included *Blue Ocean Strategy* on the reading list for his courses in order to emphasize the importance of product differentiation.[3]

The Lean LaunchPad framework stresses customer discovery—a process that encourages entrepreneurs to pause before they create a new business model. The essential first step in customer discovery involves taking time to ask existing customers what they look for in a potential new product and how they would use it. This approach differs from traditional entrepreneurship frameworks, and there are some strong parallels between the process of discovering blue oceans* that Kim and Mauborgne describe and the customer discovery process that Blank champions. By going directly to the customer, entrepreneurs can discover unmet and otherwise unseen needs, and thus unlock new markets. As Blank describes his motivation for the framework: "Business schools teach aspiring executives a variety of courses around the execution of known business models (accounting, organizational behavior, managerial skills, marketing, operations, etc.). In contrast, start-ups search for a business model. (Or more accurately, start-ups are a temporary organization designed to search for a scalable and repeatable business model.)"[4]

Summary

Students in many different disciplines will benefit from reading *Blue Ocean Strategy*. The most obvious audience is business students, who will not only discover a compelling and popular approach to strategy, but will also acquaint themselves with the debates surrounding one of the most important questions in business: how can companies differentiate themselves and grow when markets are crowded? As many business graduates seek careers in start-up companies or other alternative sectors—or even start their own companies—the core concepts of *Blue Ocean Strategy* will likely serve them well. In particular, the book's frameworks for differentiation will give students the proper tools to assess the current business landscape and grasp emerging trends.

Non-business students can benefit from the book as well, as its ideas may help them define their own careers in terms of a blue ocean paradigm. As wave after wave of students graduate college, job markets flood: graduates must differentiate themselves in order to succeed. By studying how blue oceans work and closely considering the success stories in the book, students will make better decisions about which jobs to seek and how to acquire skills that will distinguish themselves in those jobs.

NOTES

1   Ram Charan and Noel M. Tichy, *Every Business is a Growth Business: How Your Company Can Prosper Year After Year* (New York: Random House, 1998); Jonas Ridderstråle and Kjell Nordström, *Funky Business: Talent Makes Capital Dance* (Financial Times/Prentice Hall, 2007); Philip Kotler and Fernando Trías de Bes, *Lateral Marketing: New Techniques for Finding Breakthrough Ideas* (Hoboken: John Wiley & Sons, 2003); Adrian Slywotzky et al., *How to Grow When Markets Don't* (New York: Warner Business Books, 2003).

2   Steve Blank, "How to Build a Startup: The Lean LaunchPad," *Udacity*, accessed June 19, 2015, https://www.udacity.com/course/how-to-build-a-startup–ep245.

3   Steve Blank, "The Lean LaunchPad—Teaching Entrepreneurship as a Management Science," accessed June 19, 2015, http://steveblank. com/2010/12/07/the-lean-launchpad-%E2%80%93-teaching-entrepreneurship-as-a-management-science/.

4   Blank, "The Lean LaunchPad—Teaching Entrepreneurship as a Management Science," accessed June 18, 2015.

GLOSSARY

GLOSSARY OF TERMS

AltaVista: a popular search engine in the early days of the Internet. It was founded in 1995, but lost ground to Google and was purchased by Yahoo! in 2003.

Apple: founded in 1976, Apple Inc. was first created to sell personal computers. It has now grown into a publicly traded multinational technology company providing a wide range of products from software to consumer goods.

A. T. Kearney: with global offices in over 40 countries, A. T. Kearney is a management consulting firm focused on strategy and business operations. Its industry is broad, ranging from aerospace engineering to healthcare to the public sector.

The Boston Consulting Group (BCG): is a management consulting firm providing services across a wide range of industries with global offices across 46 countries. It was ranked among the best firms to work for in 2015.

Blue oceans: also known as demand creation or untapped market space, where there is opportunity for highly profitable growth.

Box (Box.com): headed by Aaron Levie, Box is a publicly traded company offering online services in the file-sharing and cloud-based computing sector.

Business strategy: when well defined, a business strategy can determine the direction of a business, with a focus on the future and business growth.

Capitalism: very roughly, the social and economic system in which business, and the profits those businesses make, is held in private hands.

Cirque du Soleil: a circus that merged theatre with circus performance founded by Montreal-based street performers Gilles Ste-Croix and Guy Laliberté. They have won numerous awards including the Rose d'Or and four Primetime Emmy Awards.

Cold Spots: areas in a business's practice that can only be improved through a significant investment in resources.

Competition: this is what happens when firms challenge each other to gain customers, market penetration, and/or branding.

Demand: in economics, demand refers to the utility for goods or services relative to a consumer's income.

First-mover advantage: the advantage acquired by the first company to enter a market, often resulting in unchallenged access to market resources (until competitors follow).

Five Forces Strategy: developed by the business strategy scholar Michael Porter, the Five Forces Strategy is designed to offer strategic tools to a business seeking to reconsider its approach to its customary market. The five forces are: threat of new entrants; threat of substitute products or services; bargaining power of customers; bargaining power of suppliers; intensity of competitive rivalry.

Generic Strategies: an approach to business strategy proposed by the business strategist Michael Porter, according to which a company considering the question of competition in its customary market must choose to follow one of three possible strategic approaches—cost leadership, differentiation, or focus—or else waste resources.

Globalization: refers to a rise in cultural integration due to greater exchange in world views and ideas globally.

Google: founded by two Stanford alumni, Larry Page and Sergey Brin, Google is the primary tool for Internet search optimization in much of the world. Its main revenue comes from advertising from searches, which are estimated to run over one billion results per day.

Horse Trading: a process of trading excess capacity (when actual production is less than optimal for a firm) between departments to obtain maximum impact within the organization.

Hot Spots: areas in a company in which a relatively small investment of resources can have a significant positive impact.

HubSpot: founded by Brian Halligan, HubSpot is a software company based in Massachussetts, focused on inbound marketing (a term coined by Brian Halligan typically referring to small businesses utilizing multiple channels—blogs, video, newsletters, social media— to attract customers through all stages of purchasing).

INSEAD Blue Ocean Strategy Institute: a global institute founded in 2007 by professors W. Chan Kim and Renée Mauborgne based on ten years of research on "blue oceans" and how best to create new markets where they did not previously exist. The institute hosts Executive Fellows each year from around the world.

INSEAD: founded in 1957, INSEAD is an international business school with campuses located in France, Asia, and the Middle East. Its degree offerings include an MBA, Executive MBA, Master in Finance and PhD.

Lean LaunchPad: an entrepreneurship model developed by Steve Blank. Rather than focus on a product, Blank emphasizes that what is key for a start-up is understanding, among other things, its customers, distribution channels, and pricing.

Market saturation: a number of different factors can cause market saturation, when a product is fully distributed across a market. These may include, but are not limited to, existing competitors, pricing, and technology.

Monopoly: when a specific person or enterprise is the only supplier of a particular commodity.

MP3: an audio coding format for digital audio for consumer audio streaming or storage.

Multidisciplinary Action Projects approach (MAP): the Multidisciplinary Action Projects associated with the Ross School of Business at the University of Michigan is an approach to action-oriented learning in which individuals work with scholars and organizations to carry out real-world projects.

New Growth Theory: a theory based on the premise that innovation is a non-scarce resource, and that growth will continue so long as innovation takes place. The theory attempts to understand innovation from an endogenous perspective; in other words, how innovation emerged from the demographic institutional conditions in an economy.

New market development: a strategy approach to growing new market segments around products.

Price wars: commercial competition characterized by the repeated cutting of prices below those of competitors.

Product differentiation: differentiation is the process of distinguishing a product from its competitors and a firm's own products through branding, promotion, by adjusting the feature set, or creating derivative products through blue ocean methodology. Differentiation is one way for companies to create long-lasting relationships with customers.

Profit: refers to the revenue remaining when a business has accounted for its costs, including taxes. It is widely assumed that the objective of a business should be to maximize profit.

Reconstructionist: Kim and Mauborgne trace the origins of the reconstructionist view to Joseph Schumpeter's theory of innovation. They argue that entrepreneurs possess the agency to change and grow markets from within; they believe innovation inside a market can be replicated once its patterns are identified.

Red Bull: a popular energy drink company, created in 1987, which combines caffeine with a number of vitamins for alertness and energy. Red Bull is the highest-selling energy drink in the world according to market share.

Red oceans: where structural conditions within an industry are considered fixed and rival firms have no choice but to compete with each other for market share.

Risk: in economics, the potential of losing something of value.

Ross School of Business: based in Michigan State, the Ross School of Business is the business school at the University of Michigan. Its motto reads, "Developing leaders who make a positive difference in the world." Ross School of Business is known for its curriculum emphasizing practical education rooted in the real world.

Second-mover advantage: the advantage that a company has when it offers a product or service later than a competitor.

Supply: the amount of a resource available in a market exchange.

Southwest Airlines: founded in 1967, Southwest Airlines is a major low-cost carrier for American flights headquartered in Texas.

Structuralism: a view of market boundaries as given and unchangeable. Structuralist roots can be traced to industrial organisation economics, where market forces (that is, supply and demand) act as determinants for buyers' and sellers' conduct. According to the authors, structuralists believe that only forces external to the market (for example, changes in government regulation, cultural movements) can alter a market's structure or boundaries.

Value creation: creating value for goods and services within a business (this can pertain to both customers and shareholders).

Value-cost trade-off: the trade-off between the value of a strategic move gained and the cost of its loss.

Value innovation: the attempt to identify and build the aspects of a business that make it competitive.

Venture capitalism: seed money invested in early-stage and emerging companies. Venture capital funds invest in companies in exchange for equity.

World Economic Forum: a Swiss public-private partnership, the World Economic Forum gathers leaders around the world to discuss global agendas. Their stated mission is "committed to improving the state of the world."

Yahoo!: founded in 1994 by Jerry Yang and David Filo, Yahoo! is an American tech company known for its web search engine, email, and other related services.

Yellow Tail: a wine brand, stylized "[yellow tail]," produced by the Australian wine producer Casella Wines, and the subject of one of the case studies presented in W. Chan Kim and Renée Mauborgne's *Blue Ocean Strategy*.

Zero-sum game: a concept in game theory describing situations in which one person's gain is another's loss.

PEOPLE MENTIONED IN THE TEXT

Steve Blank (b. 1953) is a serial entrepreneur and professor of Entrepreneurship across the US, known for promoting the Lean LaunchPad approach to entrepreneurship. His latest book, *The Startup Owner's Manual*, co-authored with Bob Dorf, draws from over 10 years of building tech companies.

Bernard Buisson is a full-time professor in France at École de Management Léonard de Vinci. He co-wrote the book *Blue Ocean or Fast-second Innovation? A Four-breakthrough Model to Explain Successful Market Domination* with Philippe Silberzahn.

Alfred Chandler, Jr. (1918–2007) was a professor of business history at Johns Hopkins University and Harvard University, and won the Pulitzer Prize in History for his research on scaling business and management practices.

Rob Coneybeer is the managing director of Shasta Ventures, an early-stage boutique venture firm in Silicon Valley investing in its fourth fund in enterprise and consumer technology start-ups.

James C. Collins (b. 1958) is a businessman, writer and managerial consultant whose teachings focus on business growth and sustainability. He is perhaps best known for his references to a "Level 5 Leader," which describes the key characteristics of a leader.

Andrejs Čirjevskis is a professor and author who received his MBA from the Riga International School of Economics and Business Administration, Latvia.

Tim Ferriss (b. 1977) is an entrepreneur, angel investor, author of several self-help books, and pubic speaker. He is best known for his popular book *The 4-Hour Work Week*, which provides advice for individuals to maximize their efficiency and build personal value.

Brian Halligan (b. 1967) is the founder of HubSpot, an Internet marketing firm, and a lecturer at Massachusetts Institute of Technology. He is a graduate of the University of Vermont and the MIT Sloan School of Management.

Gary Hamel (b. 1954) is an author, public speaker, and management consultant, the CEO of Strategos and a leader in business strategy. He is most known for originating the concept of core competencies, or the factors that contribute to a company's competitiveness.

Les Kollegian is president of She's a Competitor, Inc. and CEO of the design and branding agency Jacob Tyler.

Philip Kotler (b. 1931) is a business consultant with a focus on marketing, and the author of 55 books on strategic marketing. He is currently a business professor of international marketing at Northwestern University, Illinois.

John Kotter (b. 1947) is a management consultant, educator, and author. Kotter is the professor of leadership, emeritus at Harvard Business School and the author of 19 books, most notably *Leading Change* (1996), which presents an eight-step model for transforming organizations.

Aaron Levie (b.1985) is an entrepreneur and the founder and CEO of Box.com, an enterprise cloud company that in 2014 had 39,000 paying corporate customers.

Kjell Nordström (b. 1958) is a Swedish economist, writer, and public speaker.

Thomas J. "Tom" Peters (b. 1942) is an American author noted for his work on business management practices.

Petri Parvinen is a visiting scholar at Stanford University and a professor at the Helsinki School of Economics.

Jerry I. Porras (b. 1938) is a business and management analyst, and a professor at Stanford University's School of Business. He co-authored the book *Success Built to Last: Creating a Life That Matters.*

Michael Porter (b. 1947) is an author and professor at Harvard Business School, most widely known for his research on competitive strategy. He coined the terms the Porter Hypothesis and Porter's Five Forces in competitiveness and he is a graduate of Princeton and Harvard Business School.

C. K. Prahalad (1941–2010) was the Paul and Ruth McCracken Distinguished University Professor of Corporate Strategy at the Stephen M. Ross School of Business at the University of Michigan, US.

Jonas Ridderstråle (b. 1966) is a Swedish business thinker and public speaker, best known for co-authoring the book *Funky Business: Talent Makes Capital Dance.* He is a graduate of the Institute of International Business at the Stockholm School of Economics.

Michael Roberto is an author and business consultant on leadership, competitive strategy, and decision making, and is currently a professor of management at Bryant University in Rhode Island. Prior to that he taught at Harvard Business School for six years. He is the author of *Why Great Leaders Don't Take Yes for An Answer* (2005).

Paul Michael Romer (b. 1955) is an economist and entrepreneur. Professor of economics at the Stern School of Business at New York University, he is the author of several influential books on economic theory.

Joseph Schumpeter (1883–1950) was a prominent twentieth-century Austrian American economist and political scientist who was one of the first to theorize on entrepreneurship and innovation, coining the phrase "creative destruction" in reference to market economies that simultaneously create and destroy economic institutions. Schumpeter believed that a nation's progress stems from entrepreneurs, or wild spirits.

Philippe Silberzahn is a former research associate at INSEAD, a professor at EMLYON Business School and a research fellow at École Polytechnique, teaching courses on strategy, innovation and entrepreneurship with a focus on risk and uncertainty.

Adrian Slywotzky (b. 1951) is a business consultant and currently a partner at Oliver Wyman. He graduated from Harvard Law School and Harvard Business School and writes on business management and economic theory.

Sun Tzu (544–496 B.C.E.) was a Chinese military general, strategist, and philosopher best known for his book *The Art of War.*

Fernando Trías de Bes (b. 1967) is a writer and Spanish economist specializing in commerce, creativity and innovation.

Jorge Vasconcellos e Sá is guest lecturer at SBS Swiss Business School.

Robert H. Waterman, Jr. (b. 1936) is an author noted for his work on business management practices. He is on the board of the World Wildlife Fund and is perhaps best known as the co-author of the bestselling *In Search of Excellence: Lessons from America's Best-run Companies* (1982).

Frederick Winslow Taylor (1856–1915) was an American mechanical engineer and one of the forefathers of industrial engineering, known for his research in the efficiency movement (a movement that emerged in the early 1900s valuing efficiencies over waste in all areas of an economy—social, economic, mechanical, personal). He is the author of the book *The Principles of Scientific Management,* which was one of the first to introduce the idea of managing for efficiency.

WORKS CITED

WORKS CITED

Aurik, Johan, Gillis Jonk, and Martin Fabel, "The History of Strategy and its Future Prospects," *A. T. Kearney*, accessed June 15, 2015, https://www.atkearney.com/documents/10192/4260571/History+of+Strategy +and+Its+ Future+Prospects.pdf/29f8c6e8-7cdb -4a25-8acc-b0c39e4439e1.

Blue Ocean Strategy Institute. "Awards." Accessed October 8, 2013. http://www.blueoceanstrategy.com/awards/.

Buisson, Bernard, and Philippe Silberzahn. "Blue Ocean or Fast-second Innovation? A Four-breakthrough Model to Explain Successful Market Domination." *International Journal of Innovation Management* 14 (2010): 359–78.

Chandler, Alfred. *Strategy and Structure: Chapters in the History of the American Industrial Enterprise.* Washington, DC: Beard Books, 1962.

Charan, Ram, and Noel M. Tichy. *Every Business is a Growth Business: How Your Company Can Prosper Year After Year.* New York: Random House, 1998.

Čirjevskis, Andrejs, Genadijs Homenko, and Val rija Lačinova. "New Approaches in Measuring and Assessing Viability of Blue Ocean Strategy in B2B Sector." *Journal of Business Management* 3 (2010): 162–79.

Collins, James C., and Jerry I. Porras. *Built to Last: Successful Habits of Visionary Companies*. New York: Harper Business, 1994.

Crainer, Stuart. "W. Chan Kim and Renée Mauborgne: The Thought Leader Interview." Accessed October 8, 2013. http://www.strategy-business.com/article/11695?gko=d33f3.

Golder, Peter N., and Gerard J. Tellis. "Pioneer Advantage: Marketing Logic or Marketing Legend?" *Journal of Marketing Research* 30 (1993): 158–70.

INSEAD business school. "Blue Ocean Strategy Courses." Accessed October 29, 2013. http://www.insead.edu/blueoceanstrategyinstitute/MBA/courses.cfm.

INSEAD business school. "Blue Ocean Strategy Institute." Accessed October 29, 2013. http://knowledge.insead.edu/strategy/inseads-global-thought-leaders-w-chan-kim-and-renee-mauborgne-2938.

Kim, W. Chan, and Renée Mauborgne. *Blue Ocean Strategy: How to Create Uncontested Market Space and Make the Competition Irrelevant.* Boston: Harvard Business Press, 2005.

Kotler, Philip, and Fernando Trías de Bes. *Lateral Marketing: New Techniques for Finding Breakthrough Ideas*. Hoboken: John Wiley & Sons, 2003.

Kotter, John P., *Leading Change.* Harvard Business Review Press, 1996.

Kumar, Satheesh. "Blue Ocean Strategy: How to Create Uncontested Market Space and Make the Competition Irrelevant." *South Asian Journal of Management* 15 (2008): 121–4.

Layton, Sarah. "Blue Ocean Strategy: How to Create Uncontested Market Space and Make the Competition Irrelevant." *Consulting to Management* 16 (2005): 57–9.

Markides, Constantinos C., and Paul A. Geroski. *Fast Second: How Smart Companies Bypass Radical Innovation to Enter and Dominate New Markets.* San Francisco: Jossey-Bass, 2005.

University of Michigan's Ross School of Business, Multidisciplinary Action Projects (MAP). Accessed October 22, 2013. www.bus.umich.edu/MAP/Dev/WhatisMAP.htm.

Park, Daewoo, Mina Lee, James Turner, and Lynda Kilbourne. "Effects of Market Boundaries and Market Competition on Business Strategy in the United States Banking Sector." *International Journal of Management* 28 (2011): 363–8.

Parvinen, Petri, Jaakko Aspara, Joel Hietanen, and Sami Kajalo. "Awareness, Action and Context-specificity of Blue Ocean Practices in Sales Management." *Management Decision* 49 (2011): 1218–34.

Peters, Thomas J., and Robert H. Waterman, Jr. *In Search of Excellence: Lessons from America's Best-run Companies.* New York: Harper & Row, 1982.

Pitta, Dennis. "Issues in a Down Economy: Blue Oceans and New Product Development." *Journal of Product and Brand Management* 18 (2009): 292–6.

Porter, Michael E. *Competitive Strategy: Techniques for Analyzing Industries and Competitors.* New York: Free Press, 1980.

———.*Competitive Advantage: Creating and Sustaining Superior Performance.* New York: Free Press, 1985.

Prahalad, C. K., and Gary Hamel. "The Core Competence of the Corporation." *Harvard Business Review* (May-June 1990).

Ridderstråle, Jonas, and Kjell Nordström. *Funky Business: Talent Makes Capital Dance.* Financial Times/Prentice Hall, 2007.

Roberto, Michael. "Curves: Not Such a Blue Ocean After All." Accessed June 18 and June 19, 2015. http://michael-roberto.blogspot.com/2010/07/curves-not-such-blue-ocean-after-all.html.

Romer, Paul. "The Origins of Endogenous Growth." *Journal of Economic Perspectives* 8 (1994): 3–22.

Schumpeter, Joseph A. *Capitalism, Socialism and Democracy.* London: Taylor and Francis, 1942.

Slywotzky, Adrian, Richard Wise, with Karl Weber. *How to Grow When Markets Don't.* New York: Warner Business Books, 2003.

Tzu, Sun. "The Art of War." Project Gutenberg (1994): chapter 7, Sun-Tzu Reference Archive (2000), www.marxists.org/reference/archive/sun-tzu/works/art-of-war/ch07.htm.

Yang, Jen-te. "Identifying the Attributes of Blue Ocean Strategy in Hospitality." *International Journal of Contemporary Hospitality Management* 24 (2012): 701–20.

Wubben, Emiel F. M., Simon Düsseldorf, and Maarten H. Batterink. "Finding Uncontested Markets for European Fruit and Vegetables Through Applying the Blue Ocean Strategy." *British Food Journal* 114 (2012): 248–71.

THE MACAT LIBRARY
BY DISCIPLINE

AFRICANA STUDIES

Chinua Achebe's *An Image of Africa: Racism in Conrad's Heart of Darkness*
W. E. B. Du Bois's *The Souls of Black Folk*
Zora Neale Huston's *Characteristics of Negro Expression*
Martin Luther King Jr's *Why We Can't Wait*
Toni Morrison's *Playing in the Dark: Whiteness in the American Literary Imagination*

ANTHROPOLOGY

Arjun Appadurai's *Modernity at Large: Cultural Dimensions of Globalisation*
Philippe Ariès's *Centuries of Childhood*
Franz Boas's *Race, Language and Culture*
Kim Chan & Renée Mauborgne's *Blue Ocean Strategy*
Jared Diamond's *Guns, Germs & Steel: the Fate of Human Societies*
Jared Diamond's *Collapse: How Societies Choose to Fail or Survive*
E. E. Evans-Pritchard's *Witchcraft, Oracles and Magic Among the Azande*
James Ferguson's *The Anti-Politics Machine*
Clifford Geertz's *The Interpretation of Cultures*
David Graeber's *Debt: the First 5000 Years*
Karen Ho's *Liquidated: An Ethnography of Wall Street*
Geert Hofstede's *Culture's Consequences: Comparing Values, Behaviors, Institutes and Organizations across Nations*
Claude Lévi-Strauss's *Structural Anthropology*
Jay Macleod's *Ain't No Makin' It: Aspirations and Attainment in a Low-Income Neighborhood*
Saba Mahmood's *The Politics of Piety: The Islamic Revival and the Feminist Subject*
Marcel Mauss's *The Gift*

BUSINESS

Jean Lave & Etienne Wenger's *Situated Learning*
Theodore Levitt's *Marketing Myopia*
Burton G. Malkiel's *A Random Walk Down Wall Street*
Douglas McGregor's *The Human Side of Enterprise*
Michael Porter's *Competitive Strategy: Creating and Sustaining Superior Performance*
John Kotter's *Leading Change*
C. K. Prahalad & Gary Hamel's *The Core Competence of the Corporation*

CRIMINOLOGY

Michelle Alexander's *The New Jim Crow: Mass Incarceration in the Age of Colorblindness*
Michael R. Gottfredson & Travis Hirschi's *A General Theory of Crime*
Richard Herrnstein & Charles A. Murray's *The Bell Curve: Intelligence and Class Structure in American Life*
Elizabeth Loftus's *Eyewitness Testimony*
Jay Macleod's *Ain't No Makin' It: Aspirations and Attainment in a Low-Income Neighborhood*
Philip Zimbardo's *The Lucifer Effect*

ECONOMICS

Janet Abu-Lughod's *Before European Hegemony*
Ha-Joon Chang's *Kicking Away the Ladder*
David Brion Davis's *The Problem of Slavery in the Age of Revolution*
Milton Friedman's *The Role of Monetary Policy*
Milton Friedman's *Capitalism and Freedom*
David Graeber's *Debt: the First 5000 Years*
Friedrich Hayek's *The Road to Serfdom*
Karen Ho's *Liquidated: An Ethnography of Wall Street*

The Macat Library By Discipline

John Maynard Keynes's *The General Theory of Employment, Interest and Money*
Charles P. Kindleberger's *Manias, Panics and Crashes*
Robert Lucas's *Why Doesn't Capital Flow from Rich to Poor Countries?*
Burton G. Malkiel's *A Random Walk Down Wall Street*
Thomas Robert Malthus's *An Essay on the Principle of Population*
Karl Marx's *Capital*
Thomas Piketty's *Capital in the Twenty-First Century*
Amartya Sen's *Development as Freedom*
Adam Smith's *The Wealth of Nations*
Nassim Nicholas Taleb's *The Black Swan: The Impact of the Highly Improbable*
Amos Tversky's & Daniel Kahneman's *Judgment under Uncertainty: Heuristics and Biases*
Mahbub Ul Haq's *Reflections on Human Development*
Max Weber's *The Protestant Ethic and the Spirit of Capitalism*

FEMINISM AND GENDER STUDIES

Judith Butler's *Gender Trouble*
Simone De Beauvoir's *The Second Sex*
Michel Foucault's *History of Sexuality*
Betty Friedan's *The Feminine Mystique*
Saba Mahmood's *The Politics of Piety: The Islamic Revival and the Feminist Subject*
Joan Wallach Scott's *Gender and the Politics of History*
Mary Wollstonecraft's *A Vindication of the Rights of Woman*
Virginia Woolf's *A Room of One's Own*

GEOGRAPHY

The Brundtland Report's *Our Common Future*
Rachel Carson's *Silent Spring*
Charles Darwin's *On the Origin of Species*
James Ferguson's *The Anti-Politics Machine*
Jane Jacobs's *The Death and Life of Great American Cities*
James Lovelock's *Gaia: A New Look at Life on Earth*
Amartya Sen's *Development as Freedom*
Mathis Wackernagel & William Rees's *Our Ecological Footprint*

HISTORY

Janet Abu-Lughod's *Before European Hegemony*
Benedict Anderson's *Imagined Communities*
Bernard Bailyn's *The Ideological Origins of the American Revolution*
Hanna Batatu's *The Old Social Classes And The Revolutionary Movements Of Iraq*
Christopher Browning's *Ordinary Men: Reserve Police Batallion 101 and the Final Solution in Poland*
Edmund Burke's *Reflections on the Revolution in France*
William Cronon's *Nature's Metropolis: Chicago And The Great West*
Alfred W. Crosby's *The Columbian Exchange*
Hamid Dabashi's *Iran: A People Interrupted*
David Brion Davis's *The Problem of Slavery in the Age of Revolution*
Nathalie Zemon Davis's *The Return of Martin Guerre*
Jared Diamond's *Guns, Germs & Steel: the Fate of Human Societies*
Frank Dikotter's *Mao's Great Famine*
John W Dower's *War Without Mercy: Race And Power In The Pacific War*
W. E. B. Du Bois's *The Souls of Black Folk*
Richard J. Evans's *In Defence of History*
Lucien Febvre's *The Problem of Unbelief in the 16th Century*
Sheila Fitzpatrick's *Everyday Stalinism*

Eric Foner's *Reconstruction: America's Unfinished Revolution, 1863-1877*
Michel Foucault's *Discipline and Punish*
Michel Foucault's *History of Sexuality*
Francis Fukuyama's *The End of History and the Last Man*
John Lewis Gaddis's *We Now Know: Rethinking Cold War History*
Ernest Gellner's *Nations and Nationalism*
Eugene Genovese's *Roll, Jordan, Roll: The World the Slaves Made*
Carlo Ginzburg's *The Night Battles*
Daniel Goldhagen's *Hitler's Willing Executioners*
Jack Goldstone's *Revolution and Rebellion in the Early Modern World*
Antonio Gramsci's *The Prison Notebooks*
Alexander Hamilton, John Jay & James Madison's *The Federalist Papers*
Christopher Hill's *The World Turned Upside Down*
Carole Hillenbrand's *The Crusades: Islamic Perspectives*
Thomas Hobbes's *Leviathan*
Eric Hobsbawm's *The Age Of Revolution*
John A. Hobson's *Imperialism: A Study*
Albert Hourani's *History of the Arab Peoples*
Samuel P. Huntington's *The Clash of Civilizations and the Remaking of World Order*
C. L. R. James's *The Black Jacobins*
Tony Judt's *Postwar: A History of Europe Since 1945*
Ernst Kantorowicz's *The King's Two Bodies: A Study in Medieval Political Theology*
Paul Kennedy's *The Rise and Fall of the Great Powers*
Ian Kershaw's *The "Hitler Myth": Image and Reality in the Third Reich*
John Maynard Keynes's *The General Theory of Employment, Interest and Money*
Charles P. Kindleberger's *Manias, Panics and Crashes*
Martin Luther King Jr's *Why We Can't Wait*
Henry Kissinger's *World Order: Reflections on the Character of Nations and the Course of History*
Thomas Kuhn's *The Structure of Scientific Revolutions*
Georges Lefebvre's *The Coming of the French Revolution*
John Locke's *Two Treatises of Government*
Niccolò Machiavelli's *The Prince*
Thomas Robert Malthus's *An Essay on the Principle of Population*
Mahmood Mamdani's *Citizen and Subject: Contemporary Africa And The Legacy Of Late Colonialism*
Karl Marx's *Capital*
Stanley Milgram's *Obedience to Authority*
John Stuart Mill's *On Liberty*
Thomas Paine's *Common Sense*
Thomas Paine's *Rights of Man*
Geoffrey Parker's *Global Crisis: War, Climate Change and Catastrophe in the Seventeenth Century*
Jonathan Riley-Smith's *The First Crusade and the Idea of Crusading*
Jean-Jacques Rousseau's *The Social Contract*
Joan Wallach Scott's *Gender and the Politics of History*
Theda Skocpol's *States and Social Revolutions*
Adam Smith's *The Wealth of Nations*
Timothy Snyder's *Bloodlands: Europe Between Hitler and Stalin*
Sun Tzu's *The Art of War*
Keith Thomas's *Religion and the Decline of Magic*
Thucydides's *The History of the Peloponnesian War*
Frederick Jackson Turner's *The Significance of the Frontier in American History*
Odd Arne Westad's *The Global Cold War: Third World Interventions And The Making Of Our Times*

LITERATURE

Chinua Achebe's *An Image of Africa: Racism in Conrad's Heart of Darkness*
Roland Barthes's *Mythologies*
Homi K. Bhabha's *The Location of Culture*
Judith Butler's *Gender Trouble*
Simone De Beauvoir's *The Second Sex*
Ferdinand De Saussure's *Course in General Linguistics*
T. S. Eliot's *The Sacred Wood: Essays on Poetry and Criticism*
Zora Neale Huston's *Characteristics of Negro Expression*
Toni Morrison's *Playing in the Dark: Whiteness in the American Literary Imagination*
Edward Said's *Orientalism*
Gayatri Chakravorty Spivak's *Can the Subaltern Speak?*
Mary Wollstonecraft's *A Vindication of the Rights of Women*
Virginia Woolf's *A Room of One's Own*

PHILOSOPHY

Elizabeth Anscombe's *Modern Moral Philosophy*
Hannah Arendt's *The Human Condition*
Aristotle's *Metaphysics*
Aristotle's *Nicomachean Ethics*
Edmund Gettier's *Is Justified True Belief Knowledge?*
Georg Wilhelm Friedrich Hegel's *Phenomenology of Spirit*
David Hume's *Dialogues Concerning Natural Religion*
David Hume's *The Enquiry for Human Understanding*
Immanuel Kant's *Religion within the Boundaries of Mere Reason*
Immanuel Kant's *Critique of Pure Reason*
Søren Kierkegaard's *The Sickness Unto Death*
Søren Kierkegaard's *Fear and Trembling*
C. S. Lewis's *The Abolition of Man*
Alasdair MacIntyre's *After Virtue*
Marcus Aurelius's *Meditations*
Friedrich Nietzsche's *On the Genealogy of Morality*
Friedrich Nietzsche's *Beyond Good and Evil*
Plato's *Republic*
Plato's *Symposium*
Jean-Jacques Rousseau's *The Social Contract*
Gilbert Ryle's *The Concept of Mind*
Baruch Spinoza's *Ethics*
Sun Tzu's *The Art of War*
Ludwig Wittgenstein's *Philosophical Investigations*

POLITICS

Benedict Anderson's *Imagined Communities*
Aristotle's *Politics*
Bernard Bailyn's *The Ideological Origins of the American Revolution*
Edmund Burke's *Reflections on the Revolution in France*
John C. Calhoun's *A Disquisition on Government*
Ha-Joon Chang's *Kicking Away the Ladder*
Hamid Dabashi's *Iran: A People Interrupted*
Hamid Dabashi's *Theology of Discontent: The Ideological Foundation of the Islamic Revolution in Iran*
Robert Dahl's *Democracy and its Critics*
Robert Dahl's *Who Governs?*
David Brion Davis's *The Problem of Slavery in the Age of Revolution*

Alexis De Tocqueville's *Democracy in America*
James Ferguson's *The Anti-Politics Machine*
Frank Dikotter's *Mao's Great Famine*
Sheila Fitzpatrick's *Everyday Stalinism*
Eric Foner's *Reconstruction: America's Unfinished Revolution, 1863-1877*
Milton Friedman's *Capitalism and Freedom*
Francis Fukuyama's *The End of History and the Last Man*
John Lewis Gaddis's *We Now Know: Rethinking Cold War History*
Ernest Gellner's *Nations and Nationalism*
David Graeber's *Debt: the First 5000 Years*
Antonio Gramsci's *The Prison Notebooks*
Alexander Hamilton, John Jay & James Madison's *The Federalist Papers*
Friedrich Hayek's *The Road to Serfdom*
Christopher Hill's *The World Turned Upside Down*
Thomas Hobbes's *Leviathan*
John A. Hobson's *Imperialism: A Study*
Samuel P. Huntington's *The Clash of Civilizations and the Remaking of World Order*
Tony Judt's *Postwar: A History of Europe Since 1945*
David C. Kang's *China Rising: Peace, Power and Order in East Asia*
Paul Kennedy's *The Rise and Fall of Great Powers*
Robert Keohane's *After Hegemony*
Martin Luther King Jr.'s *Why We Can't Wait*
Henry Kissinger's *World Order: Reflections on the Character of Nations and the Course of History*
John Locke's *Two Treatises of Government*
Niccolò Machiavelli's *The Prince*
Thomas Robert Malthus's *An Essay on the Principle of Population*
Mahmood Mamdani's *Citizen and Subject: Contemporary Africa And The Legacy Of Late Colonialism*
Karl Marx's *Capital*
John Stuart Mill's *On Liberty*
John Stuart Mill's *Utilitarianism*
Hans Morgenthau's *Politics Among Nations*
Thomas Paine's *Common Sense*
Thomas Paine's *Rights of Man*
Thomas Piketty's *Capital in the Twenty-First Century*
Robert D. Putman's *Bowling Alone*
John Rawls's *Theory of Justice*
Jean-Jacques Rousseau's *The Social Contract*
Theda Skocpol's *States and Social Revolutions*
Adam Smith's *The Wealth of Nations*
Sun Tzu's *The Art of War*
Henry David Thoreau's *Civil Disobedience*
Thucydides's *The History of the Peloponnesian War*
Kenneth Waltz's *Theory of International Politics*
Max Weber's *Politics as a Vocation*
Odd Arne Westad's *The Global Cold War: Third World Interventions And The Making Of Our Times*

POSTCOLONIAL STUDIES

Roland Barthes's *Mythologies*
Frantz Fanon's *Black Skin, White Masks*
Homi K. Bhabha's *The Location of Culture*
Gustavo Gutiérrez's *A Theology of Liberation*
Edward Said's *Orientalism*
Gayatri Chakravorty Spivak's *Can the Subaltern Speak?*

PSYCHOLOGY

Gordon Allport's *The Nature of Prejudice*
Alan Baddeley & Graham Hitch's *Aggression: A Social Learning Analysis*
Albert Bandura's *Aggression: A Social Learning Analysis*
Leon Festinger's *A Theory of Cognitive Dissonance*
Sigmund Freud's *The Interpretation of Dreams*
Betty Friedan's *The Feminine Mystique*
Michael R. Gottfredson & Travis Hirschi's *A General Theory of Crime*
Eric Hoffer's *The True Believer: Thoughts on the Nature of Mass Movements*
William James's *Principles of Psychology*
Elizabeth Loftus's *Eyewitness Testimony*
A. H. Maslow's *A Theory of Human Motivation*
Stanley Milgram's *Obedience to Authority*
Steven Pinker's *The Better Angels of Our Nature*
Oliver Sacks's *The Man Who Mistook His Wife For a Hat*
Richard Thaler & Cass Sunstein's *Nudge: Improving Decisions About Health, Wealth and Happiness*
Amos Tversky's *Judgment under Uncertainty: Heuristics and Biases*
Philip Zimbardo's *The Lucifer Effect*

SCIENCE

Rachel Carson's *Silent Spring*
William Cronon's *Nature's Metropolis: Chicago And The Great West*
Alfred W. Crosby's *The Columbian Exchange*
Charles Darwin's *On the Origin of Species*
Richard Dawkin's *The Selfish Gene*
Thomas Kuhn's *The Structure of Scientific Revolutions*
Geoffrey Parker's *Global Crisis: War, Climate Change and Catastrophe in the Seventeenth Century*
Mathis Wackernagel & William Rees's *Our Ecological Footprint*

SOCIOLOGY

Michelle Alexander's *The New Jim Crow: Mass Incarceration in the Age of Colorblindness*
Gordon Allport's *The Nature of Prejudice*
Albert Bandura's *Aggression: A Social Learning Analysis*
Hanna Batatu's *The Old Social Classes And The Revolutionary Movements Of Iraq*
Ha-Joon Chang's *Kicking Away the Ladder*
W. E. B. Du Bois's *The Souls of Black Folk*
Émile Durkheim's *On Suicide*
Frantz Fanon's *Black Skin, White Masks*
Frantz Fanon's *The Wretched of the Earth*
Eric Foner's *Reconstruction: America's Unfinished Revolution, 1863-1877*
Eugene Genovese's *Roll, Jordan, Roll: The World the Slaves Made*
Jack Goldstone's *Revolution and Rebellion in the Early Modern World*
Antonio Gramsci's *The Prison Notebooks*
Richard Herrnstein & Charles A Murray's *The Bell Curve: Intelligence and Class Structure in American Life*
Eric Hoffer's *The True Believer: Thoughts on the Nature of Mass Movements*
Jane Jacobs's *The Death and Life of Great American Cities*
Robert Lucas's *Why Doesn't Capital Flow from Rich to Poor Countries?*
Jay Macleod's *Ain't No Makin' It: Aspirations and Attainment in a Low Income Neighborhood*
Elaine May's *Homeward Bound: American Families in the Cold War Era*
Douglas McGregor's *The Human Side of Enterprise*
C. Wright Mills's *The Sociological Imagination*

Thomas Piketty's *Capital in the Twenty-First Century*
Robert D. Putman's *Bowling Alone*
David Riesman's *The Lonely Crowd: A Study of the Changing American Character*
Edward Said's *Orientalism*
Joan Wallach Scott's *Gender and the Politics of History*
Theda Skocpol's *States and Social Revolutions*
Max Weber's *The Protestant Ethic and the Spirit of Capitalism*

THEOLOGY

Augustine's *Confessions*
Benedict's *Rule of St Benedict*
Gustavo Gutiérrez's *A Theology of Liberation*
Carole Hillenbrand's *The Crusades: Islamic Perspectives*
David Hume's *Dialogues Concerning Natural Religion*
Immanuel Kant's *Religion within the Boundaries of Mere Reason*
Ernst Kantorowicz's *The King's Two Bodies: A Study in Medieval Political Theology*
Søren Kierkegaard's *The Sickness Unto Death*
C. S. Lewis's *The Abolition of Man*
Saba Mahmood's *The Politics of Piety: The Islamic Revival and the Feminist Subject*
Baruch Spinoza's *Ethics*
Keith Thomas's *Religion and the Decline of Magic*

COMING SOON

Chris Argyris's *The Individual and the Organisation*
Seyla Benhabib's *The Rights of Others*
Walter Benjamin's *The Work Of Art in the Age of Mechanical Reproduction*
John Berger's *Ways of Seeing*
Pierre Bourdieu's *Outline of a Theory of Practice*
Mary Douglas's *Purity and Danger*
Roland Dworkin's *Taking Rights Seriously*
James G. March's *Exploration and Exploitation in Organisational Learning*
Ikujiro Nonaka's *A Dynamic Theory of Organizational Knowledge Creation*
Griselda Pollock's *Vision and Difference*
Amartya Sen's *Inequality Re-Examined*
Susan Sontag's *On Photography*
Yasser Tabbaa's *The Transformation of Islamic Art*
Ludwig von Mises's *Theory of Money and Credit*

Macat Disciplines

Access the greatest ideas and thinkers across entire disciplines, including

AFRICANA STUDIES

Chinua Achebe's *An Image of Africa:*
Racism in Conrad's Heart of Darkness

W. E. B. Du Bois's *The Souls of Black Folk*

Zora Neale Hurston's *Characteristics of Negro Expression*

Martin Luther King Jr.'s *Why We Can't Wait*

Toni Morrison's *Playing in the Dark:*
Whiteness in the American Literary Imagination

Macat Disciplines

Access the greatest ideas and thinkers across entire disciplines, including

FEMINISM, GENDER AND QUEER STUDIES

Simone De Beauvoir's
The Second Sex

Michel Foucault's
History of Sexuality

Betty Friedan's
The Feminine Mystique

Saba Mahmood's
The Politics of Piety: The Islamic Revival and the Feminist Subject

Joan Wallach Scott's
Gender and the Politics of History

Mary Wollstonecraft's
A Vindication of the Rights of Woman

Virginia Woolf's
A Room of One's Own

Judith Butler's
Gender Trouble

Macat analyses are available from all good bookshops and libraries.

Access hundreds of analyses through one, multimedia tool.
Join free for one month **library.macat.com**

Macat Disciplines

Access the greatest ideas and thinkers across entire disciplines, including

INEQUALITY

Ha-Joon Chang's, *Kicking Away the Ladder*
David Graeber's, *Debt: The First 5000 Years*
Robert E. Lucas's, *Why Doesn't Capital Flow from Rich To Poor Countries?*
Thomas Piketty's, *Capital in the Twenty-First Century*
Amartya Sen's, *Inequality Re-Examined*
Mahbub Ul Haq's, *Reflections on Human Development*

Macat analyses are available from all good bookshops and libraries.

Access hundreds of analyses through one, multimedia tool.
Join free for one month **library.macat.com**

Macat Disciplines

Access the greatest ideas and thinkers across entire disciplines, including

CRIMINOLOGY

Macat Disciplines

Access the greatest ideas and thinkers across entire disciplines, including

Postcolonial Studies

Roland Barthes's *Mythologies*
Frantz Fanon's *Black Skin, White Masks*
Homi K. Bhabha's *The Location of Culture*
Gustavo Gutiérrez's *A Theology of Liberation*
Edward Said's *Orientalism*
Gayatri Chakravorty Spivak's *Can the Subaltern Speak?*

Macat analyses are available from all good bookshops and libraries.

Access hundreds of analyses through one, multimedia tool.

Join free for one month **library.macat.com**

Macat Disciplines

*Access the greatest ideas and thinkers
across entire disciplines, including*

GLOBALIZATION

Arjun Appadurai's, *Modernity at Large:
Cultural Dimensions of Globalisation*

James Ferguson's, *The Anti-Politics Machine*

Geert Hofstede's, *Culture's Consequences*

Amartya Sen's, *Development as Freedom*

Macat analyses are available from all good bookshops and libraries.

Access hundreds of analyses through one, multimedia tool.
Join free for one month **library.macat.com**

Macat Pairs

Analyse historical and modern issues from opposite sides of an argument. Pairs include:

HOW TO RUN AN ECONOMY

John Maynard Keynes's
The General Theory OF Employment, Interest and Money

Classical economics suggests that market economies are self-correcting in times of recession or depression, and tend toward full employment and output. But English economist John Maynard Keynes disagrees.

In his ground-breaking 1936 study *The General Theory*, Keynes argues that traditional economics has misunderstood the causes of unemployment. Employment is not determined by the price of labor; it is directly linked to demand. Keynes believes market economies are by nature unstable, and so require government intervention. Spurred on by the social catastrophe of the Great Depression of the 1930s, he sets out to revolutionize the way the world thinks

Milton Friedman's
The Role of Monetary Policy

Friedman's 1968 paper changed the course of economic theory. In just 17 pages, he demolished existing theory and outlined an effective alternate monetary policy designed to secure 'high employment, stable prices and rapid growth.'

Friedman demonstrated that monetary policy plays a vital role in broader economic stability and argued that economists got their monetary policy wrong in the 1950s and 1960s by misunderstanding the relationship between inflation and unemployment. Previous generations of economists had believed that governments could permanently decrease unemployment by permitting inflation—and vice versa. Friedman's most original contribution was to show that this supposed trade-off is an illusion that only works in the short term.

Macat Disciplines

Access the greatest ideas and thinkers across entire disciplines, including

THE FUTURE OF DEMOCRACY

Robert A. Dahl's, *Democracy and Its Critics*
Robert A. Dahl's, *Who Governs?*
Alexis De Toqueville's, *Democracy in America*
Niccolò Machiavelli's, *The Prince*
John Stuart Mill's, *On Liberty*
Robert D. Putnam's, *Bowling Alone*
Jean-Jacques Rousseau's, *The Social Contract*
Henry David Thoreau's, *Civil Disobedience*

Macat analyses are available from all good bookshops and libraries.

Access hundreds of analyses through one, multimedia tool.
Join free for one month **library.macat.com**

Macat Disciplines

Access the greatest ideas and thinkers across entire disciplines, including

TOTALITARIANISM

Sheila Fitzpatrick's, *Everyday Stalinism*
Ian Kershaw's, *The "Hitler Myth"*
Timothy Snyder's, *Bloodlands*

Macat analyses are available from all good bookshops and libraries.

Access hundreds of analyses through one, multimedia tool.
Join free for one month **library.macat.com**

Macat Pairs

Analyse historical and modern issues from opposite sides of an argument. Pairs include:

Zora Neale Hurston's
Characteristics of Negro Expression

Using material collected on anthropological expeditions to the South, Zora Neale Hurston explains how expression in African American culture in the early twentieth century departs from the art of white America. At the time, African American art was often criticized for copying white culture. For Hurston, this criticism misunderstood how art works. European tradition views art as something fixed. But Hurston describes a creative process that is alive, ever-changing, and largely improvisational. She maintains that African American art works through a process called 'mimicry'—where an imitated object or verbal pattern, for example, is reshaped and altered until it becomes something new, novel—and worthy of attention.

Frantz Fanon's
Black Skin, White Masks

Black Skin, White Masks offers a radical analysis of the psychological effects of colonization on the colonized.

Fanon witnessed the effects of colonization first hand both in his birthplace, Martinique, and again later in life when he worked as a psychiatrist in another French colony, Algeria. His text is uncompromising in form and argument. He dissects the dehumanizing effects of colonialism, arguing that it destroys the native sense of identity, forcing people to adapt to an alien set of values—including a core belief that they are inferior. This results in deep psychological trauma.

Fanon's work played a pivotal role in the civil rights movements of the 1960s.

Macat Pairs

Analyse historical and modern issues from opposite sides of an argument. Pairs include:

INTERNATIONAL RELATIONS IN THE 21ST CENTURY

Samuel P. Huntington's
The Clash of Civilisations

In his highly influential 1996 book, Huntington offers a vision of a post-Cold War world in which conflict takes place not between competing ideologies but between cultures. The worst clash, he argues, will be between the Islamic world and the West: the West's arrogance and belief that its culture is a "gift" to the world will come into conflict with Islam's obstinacy and concern that its culture is under attack from a morally decadent "other."

Clash inspired much debate between different political schools of thought. But its greatest impact came in helping define American foreign policy in the wake of the 2001 terrorist attacks in New York and Washington.

Francis Fukuyama's
The End of History and the Last Man

Published in 1992, *The End of History and the Last Man* argues that capitalist democracy is the final destination for all societies. Fukuyama believed democracy triumphed during the Cold War because it lacks the "fundamental contradictions" inherent in communism and satisfies our yearning for freedom and equality. Democracy therefore marks the endpoint in the evolution of ideology, and so the "end of history." There will still be "events," but no fundamental change in ideology.

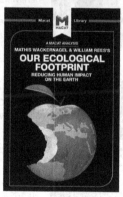

Macat Pairs

Analyse historical and modern issues from opposite sides of an argument. Pairs include:

Macat Pairs

*Analyse historical and modern issues
from opposite sides of an argument.
Pairs include:*

HOW WE RELATE TO EACH
OTHER AND SOCIETY

Jean-Jacques Rousseau's
The Social Contract

Rousseau's famous work sets out the radical concept of the 'social contract': a give-and-take relationship between individual freedom and social order.

If people are free to do as they like, governed only by their own sense of justice, they are also vulnerable to chaos and violence. To avoid this, Rousseau proposes, they should agree to give up some freedom to benefit from the protection of social and political organization. But this deal is only just if societies are led by the collective needs and desires of the people, and able to control the private interests of individuals. For Rousseau, the only legitimate form of government is rule by the people.

Robert D. Putnam's
Bowling Alone

In *Bowling Alone*, Robert Putnam argues that Americans have become disconnected from one another and from the institutions of their common life, and investigates the consequences of this change.

Looking at a range of indicators, from membership in formal organizations to the number of invitations being extended to informal dinner parties, Putnam demonstrates that Americans are interacting less and creating less "social capital" – with potentially disastrous implications for their society.

It would be difficult to overstate the impact of *Bowling Alone*, one of the most frequently cited social science publications of the last half-century.

Macat analyses are available from all good bookshops and libraries.

Access hundreds of analyses through one, multimedia tool.
Join free for one month **library.macat.com**

Printed in the United States
by Baker & Taylor Publisher Services